Praise for Donna Ferres and *Undying Will*

"It takes the rawest kind of courage to do what Donna has done. In *Undying Will* she takes a step most victims can never do—that of publicly baring her soul to reach out and help other survivors of violent rape."
—Judith D. Pulte, MA, Mental Health Counselor

"Your book is wonderfully written, gripping and emotional. I admire the way you spoke from the heart. You have attained the one purpose you have worked so hard to do and that is *making a difference.* I consider myself lucky to have purchased and have read your book. I've learned that one can restore their spirit with perseverance and courage."
—Kristi Torrico, American Airlines Pilot

"I read Donna's book and was amazed she can function with everyday life and with helping others in such a compassionate way. I gave her book to a good friend who was raped. My friend was not aware that a book written by a rape victim was available and how much it helped her. We both feel that Donna's book should be made public. Additionally, we both felt that Donna does have an *undying will.*"
—MaryEllen Carson

"Thank you ever so much for your undying will and for the positive difference you are making in so many lives. My name is Lynn and I, too, have survived violence. While my elderly parents were visiting, I purchased your book, *Undying Will*, in hopes they would read it and finally come to an understanding within themselves. THAT HAPPENED! Through the voice of the keyboard you were able to communicate to them the very things I've strived for them to understand all along. Thank you. Thank you ever so much."
—Lynn Ritter, Survivor

"Donna Ferres' strength and perseverance are an inspiration to all. I couldn't put her book down. Every page was a new adventure in learning what a rape victim feels inside. Donna refused to accept what happened to her as a disability. She continues her journey by helping rape victims."

—*Bonnie Faucette, Investigator, State of Maryland*

"Upon reading *Undying Will*, I became engulfed in Donna's vibrant use of language as she revealed to her reader, the tumultuous accounts of her experiences during and after her horrific rape. As her truly remarkable struggle to gain back her innocence, while fighting for justice, begins to unravel, I became absorbed in her accounts and it became even more riveting to me, and I was unable to put the book down until I had finished it. Being a rape survivor myself, I could not help the triggered emotions I was feeling, and was overwhelmed by the sudden rush of my own memories. Ms. Ferres was so articulate in her writing that I actually felt that I was right there with her, able to feel her every emotion. For someone who has never experienced such a treacherous event in their life they are soon able to feel what the experience was like for her, as she journeys through the accounts of that dreaded day, all the way through to the prosecution of the perpetrator. Like most victims, Donna felt scared, hurt, lonely, bitter and (sadly enough) guilty, unfortunately these are the feelings that most survivors experience. These accounts truly bring survivors' feelings to the forefront, letting others know that it is not only normal, but most of all, that it is O.K. to feel this way. It should be mentioned that for any survivor of a sexual crime this book will trigger emotions that are not felt in their everyday life and therefore should be in a *SAFE* place."

—*Marlena, Survivor, www.mrs88888.com*

"*Undying Will* reminds us not to worry about the unimportant things in life but enjoy each day to its fullest."

—*Lanny Kalpin, USPTA Tennis Professional*

"Donna's story is so real it's like a bad dream you can't wake up from. If this book doesn't make the world understand the horrors a sexual assault victim endures, I don't know what will. Ms. Ferres is a triumphantly strong woman."

—*Marianne Cushing, VP, Insight Advertising*

"*Undying Will* has impacted my life in ways that others will never know. After reading this book I was awakened to many things that had happened to me, that I had never realized were wrong. Donna Ferres tells her story in such a way that you feel every moment of pain and every moment of triumph right along with her. It took me many years to become aware of the atrocities inflicted on me that had been buried for so long. Donna's story made me feel like I wasn't alone anymore and that I need not live in shame for things over which I had no control. She is an inspiration to me every day. I will never forget the sharing of her story and forever will be grateful for the opportunity to begin to realize my own personal potential after finally releasing my own demons. She has given me the freedom to move on with my life. Donna Ferres…thank you for my future."

—*Melissa Mueller, Medical Insurance Manager*

"*Undying Will* is a moving and powerful story told from the heart of a brave and courageous woman. Ms. Ferres's strength and conviction empowers victims everywhere."

—*Alicia L. Dohn, MA, Mental Health Therapist*

"I couldn't put your book down. My husband couldn't believe what I was reading to him. A Korean War hero, he was wounded and lay bleeding and was sure he was going to die. The enemy kicked and poked him, but he lay still and did not move. He says, he prayed that God would let him live. God heard his prayers as I'm sure he called you back to life by the barking dog."

—*Eunice and Buddy Kalpin*

"After reading your book, I know that anyone who reads it will be touched in a way that will change their life. I feel so honored to know a person of such courage, perseverance and will."

—*Dr. and Mrs. Kovaz*

"Your story, *Undying Will*, really stirs up a lot of emotions. Although you may think that your book is targeted toward abuse survivors and their families, you'd be surprised at how I would think that most anyone could obtain some insight from it. You validate a lot of feelings that at least I have in my life that I thought I was alone in feeling. I have not suffered the type of horrific violence that you endured, yet I, as I would assume most people, have my own demons to deal with. As I listened to you express your wide range of emotions, I found myself repeatedly thinking, I've felt that same way. You've done a really good thing. You put yourself out there and by doing that, you showed a lot of people that they are not alone in their feelings and that they, too, can be a survivor."

—*Selena Martin, Medical Transcriptions/Mother*

"Donna Ferres is a truly remarkable person, evidenced by her will to survive and her subsequent achievements. She didn't do this alone; she had an array of assistance. Her astonishing *"journey"* was made with the help of her strong support group. It cannot be over-emphasized how important it is for a victim to be understood, supported and encouraged by family and friends. They can make such a horrific "journey" bearable."

—*Deb and Dave Harrington*

"Donna Ferres has survived an incredible trauma, both physically and mentally. Her strength has made me a better person."

—*Bev Dommerich*

"I started reading Donna's book and could not put it down. I grew up with Donna and knew her well before this tragic incident completely changed her life and her relationships with all who knew her. She went from a carefree, fun-loving person to a scared, insecure person, who became unable to continue her life as she knew it. I am just so happy to see her at this point, putting the worst thing that could happen to anyone behind her and putting her experience to helping other victims who need someone who knows what they are going through. She is finally, after many years, showing some of that carefree, fun-loving person that she was. Her book is very well written and with every page read makes you want more. Donna is a true survivor to me and all that knew her before this terrible assault."

—Dorothy Torres, *Longtime Friend*

"Donna first had to heal herself of the pain that had been inflicted upon her. Through time and patience, she has had the courage to walk forward into a world of uncertainty, never, ever knowing."

—Edith and Rocco Sangiacomo

"You have a wonderful and inspiring story about the strength and courage of a woman overcoming a tragedy that many of us will never understand. Your book, *Undying Will,* was painful to read but I know it has helped many other women who are trying to survive such an ordeal. The fact that tennis helped you gain confidence and build trust again, shows that there is life after tragedy. Tennis can be a positive addition to anyone's life. The game itself is full of challenges, fun and excitement but the best part of tennis is the people you meet associated with the sport. Tennis people are vibrant, energetic and fun-loving human beings. I am a happier and more successful person because tennis has been an important part of my life for over 22 years."

—Loretta Strickland, *USA Tennis Director*

"*Undying Will* is such an appropriate name for Ms. Ferres' book. She displays the ultimate in courage, determination and will of any individual I have ever met. The style in which it is written left me speechless and rendered me face-to-face with the reality of sexual assault. I truly felt the emotional anguish and devastation that Ms. Ferres experienced. I am honored to know her and would recommend *Undying Will*. It definitely would be an asset to any victim or family member of sexual assault."

—*Melanie Geenen, Rape Trauma Center, Inc. dba Phoenix Center*

"Although I was initially compelled to feel sadness and sympathy for Donna because she had to endure pain and suffering that someone else intentionally inflicted, I am proud to know that she intends her pain to take away pain from others, because she knows that pain too well."

—*Janet M. Couet, MA*

"Ms. Ferres honestly explores the range of emotions anyone experiences from a traumatic event. We have recommended *Undying Will* to several friends as an aid in the healing process. In times of crisis, it is helpful to know your feelings are not unusual and others experience similar emotions. This book deals with the survival of a terrible crime, the enduring emotional strength she discovered within her soul and the hope of a better life."

—*Tom and Donna Chase*

"*Undying Will* presents a story of survival, perseverance and a victim's triumph over her perpetrator. This book provides tremendous insights for families of the victim, particularly for mothers and daughters."

—*Diann Cimring, Firestone & Cimring Advertising*

"Donna's story will effect everyone. Both men and women can learn from her and become aware of how her life was changed and why."

—*Steve A. Hawks, Sr. VP Paine Webber*

"Your book, *Undying Will,* reads like a horror suspense thriller, HARD to believe that it is TRUE...yet I KNOW that it is, which made it painful to read. I can see from your afterword that you have come a long way."

—*Sharon Tobler, PhD, Clinical Psychologist*

"A candid testimony to the devastating effects of trauma and the ability to finally heal through support and perseverance."

—*Kimberly S. Crane, Licensed Mental Health Counselor*

"Ms. Ferres' book, *Undying Will,* is a testament to the indomitable nature of the human spirit. It is a study in overcoming adversity, of perseverance, of triumph over evil. Eventually Ms. Ferres was able to cut through the nonsense of lawyers and court procedures and parole hearings, too, facing her attacker and making sure he stayed in jail. And in the middle of all this, she had to reclaim her spirit, for it was more broken than her body. Most of us stumble over a few bumps in the road. Read Donna Ferres's book to put your own troubles into perspective and know that you, too, can triumph."

—*Drollene Brown, Editor*

Thank you for your interest. . .

Undying Will

A True Story of How
One Woman Survived
a Brutal Rape
and Near Murder
to Bring Her Attacker
to Justice.

Donna J. Ferres

Sago Publishing
Fort Myers, Florida

First printing 2002

ISBN 0-9710413-1-8

LCCN 2001098826

ATTENTION CORPORATIONS, UNIVERSITIES, COLLEGES, AND PROFESSIONAL ORGANIZATIONS: Quantity discounts are available on bulk purchases of this book for educational, gift purposes, or as premiums for increasing magazine subscriptions or renewals. Special books or book excerpts can also be created to fit specific needs. For information, please contact Sago Publishing, 12328 Honeysuckle Road, Fort Myers, FL 33912; ph. 941-768-0673.

This book is dedicated to all the victims who were not as fortunate as I, to have survived a brutal attack.

To the loved ones of the victims, I want to share my thoughts during what could have been the last moments of my life. I hope this will provide insight and solace for those who have lost someone to a violent attack, fearing that the end for their loved one was painful and terrifying.

My thoughts in the last moments, as I lay dying, were transformed from being scared out of my mind, believing he might come back, to a calm, peaceful state of acceptance of my death. My body became weightless, and my mind emptied, for I believed I was going to a better place; I didn't feel any pain. It was as if time stood still as I closed my eyes to die.

Then the dog barked…

TABLE OF CONTENTS

There are moments—hours, days, weeks—in the life of a survivor when having survived seems worse than death. It is for those who suffer those moments thinking they are alone that I write this book. I also write for those family members, friends, colleagues and acquaintances who are struggling to understand why the survivor does not simply "get over it."

This is the story of my surviving a brutal assault; but more than that it is the account of my surviving the aftermath— the flashbacks, the feelings of worthlessness, the thoughts of self-loathing, the guilt. For years it seemed, no sooner had I gotten myself on an even keel than something would happen to hurl me back to that one awful morning when my life was changed forever.

Here is a message of hope after despair, of light after darkness. Take this journey with me and you will see that you are not alone. Others like you have fought the fight and won. I did it; so can you.

ACKNOWLEDGMENTS

I wish to give special thanks to several people who, through it all, never gave up on me, helped me when I needed help and accepted me for the person I have become. These people never judged me or abandoned me.

I thank my sisters, Barbara and Debbie, who loved me enough and trusted me to share a part of their lives in the pages that follow and who, after all these years, still remain close. I thank you both and will forever remember all the good things you have done for me.

I thank my mother and father for bringing me up the best way they knew.

I give enormous gratitude to Roxann for the many things she has helped me with. To her I say, thank you for your loyal friendship in allowing me to share my most painful and personal events. Thank you for referring me to the best doctors and for standing by me through my worst hospitalizations. Thank you for spearheading the multiple letter-writing campaigns to the parole board. Thank you for enduring my depressed moods, fears and phobias, and thank you for being by my side when there was no one else. There is so much I want to thank you for, but what stands out most is your continued support and encouragement.

I wish to thank all the doctors and nurses at University Hospital Shock Trauma Unit, the Earleigh Heights Fire Department paramedics, the Anne Arundle County homicide detectives and prosecutor's office. I want to thank, especially, Ina Norton, my therapist at the Baltimore County Rape Crisis Center for her gentle approach to helping me deal with the attack.

I thank Roberta Roper, Director of the Stephanie Roper Committee for Victims' Rights in Maryland, for educating and advising me of my rights under Maryland law to attend my attacker's open parole hearing. Without your help, my book would have no ending. Thanks also to all those who wrote in support of me to the Parole Board, including Senator Barbara Mikulski, Governor Parris Glendening, State Attorney Frank Weathersbee and countless others.

1 En Route to Shock Trauma

"Emergency! Emergency!"

It is 5 A.M., Friday, August 3, 1979, when the call echoes over the loudspeaker. Doctors and nurses at the Shock Trauma Unit of the University Hospital now know an emergency is en route by helicopter.

The unit radio follows with a more complete message: "Twenty-four-year-old white female en route. She is suffering from multiple stab wounds, one to the chest and two to the lower torso. She has contusions to her face and upper body. Abrasions cover the entire body. Patient's vital signs are unstable. Blood pressure is low, pulse rapid, respiration 24 and shallow. Patient has allegedly been raped. Paramedics have inserted Dextrose 5 percent, .5 normal saline solution intravenously. Nasal cannula with oxygen was begun on the scene. Approximate arrival time, 5:30 A.M."

The hum of the helicopter is so loud it makes my ears pop.

"Hang in there! Hang in there!" yells the paramedic sitting next to me.

I lie flat on my back on a leather stretcher, my body covered with a heavy black metal sheet to subdue the profuse

1

bleeding. Feeling as though all the blood has drained from my body, I open my swollen eyes to focus on the source of the voice. As I lie helplessly staring up at the paramedic, wondering if he will be the last person I will ever see, I concentrate on making my lips move. With what feels like my last breath, I say, "I'm dying."

He places an oxygen mask over my nose and mouth. "You're going to be all right. Just hang in there for a few more minutes. I can see the city lights from here, and the hospital is not far." His voice is shaky as he looks forward through the front window of the helicopter.

I don't know what's keeping me alive, but I continue to breathe even though I can feel myself weakening, wanting only to go to sleep. The paramedic holds my hand. His touch is soothing and warm, an anomaly coming from such a large, stocky man. I interpret his worried expression and lack of eye contact to mean my end is near. Studying him, strangely enough, allows me to repress my own thoughts of dying. We begin to drop, and my stomach feels as though it has been left behind, a sickening sensation.

"We have touchdown," a male voice yells from the cockpit of the copter. The side door thunders open, causing my body to jump, almost disconnecting my intravenous lines. My stretcher is being pulled from the helicopter by the two paramedics, passing me to the waiting hands of the hospital staff. The humid August air hits my bruised face as the sun begins to rise, shining its dull light upon me.

Three nurses clutch the bloodied sheet under me as one nurse shouts to be heard over the sound of the hovering blades: "On three! One, two, three!" On the third count my bruised body is lifted and gently placed on a crisp white sheet covering a metal gurney. They rush me into a waiting elevator. As one, we stare up at the rounded numbers above the doors of the elevator, a beeping noise indicating our journey past each floor. The final beep sounds and the doors open.

"Go!" commands one of the women. My gurney, with nurses at the sides and front, rolls quickly into a desolate, cold hallway. For a quick moment I become disorientated. As I masticate the grit and sand between my teeth, I flash back to feeling my attacker on top of me. I try to flail my arms in defense, but the heavy metal blanket prevents me from moving.

The hall is cold and dimly lit, and the only sounds to be heard are the rolling wheels of the gurney and the squeaking sounds of sneakers against the tiled floor. The musty smell and dreary atmosphere remind me of the old military hospital in Fort Meade, Maryland, near where my career army father finally settled our family after many years of moving from state to state.

As a set of automatic doors opens, I look up to see the large red sign, "SHOCK TRAUMA," and the team rolls my gurney into a trauma room. Within seconds the place is swarming with doctors and nurses. My eyes sweep the room as people touch and roll me. One wall is lined with silver stands covered in sterile blue cloths, awaiting use. On another wall are glass jars with hoses and tubes attached; signs announce their purpose: oxygen…suction…air. A large, domed, steel—blinding!—light is directly above me. Doctors—of various specialties—loom above me, introducing themselves as they work, performing in unison to stabilize my bloodied and lacerated body and prepare me for surgery. While one doctor pokes and prods my bleeding wounds, a second doctor injects a yellow dye into the IV tube, then directs the x-ray tech to begin taking pictures. A third doctor yells orders to the surgical nursing staff.

The primary physician begins dictating his assessment. "Patient was transferred by helicopter from the scene of the assault. Patient suffers multiple stab wounds and alleged rape. There is a noted stab wound in the left upper quadrant at the midclavicular line, just below the costal margin. There are noted to be two stab wounds in the posterior aspect of the thorax above the level of the iliac on the right side. Patient arrived with a blood pressure ranging in the area of 100 mm systolic but extremely tachycardic and pale, with distended abdomen."

I am crying, thinking of those I will leave behind. *My poor family. I may never see them again.* It is my mother for whom I feel the most sadness. She has already lost one daughter. She will be devastated to lose me, too.

A few of the trauma team leave, and immediately the temperature in the room seems to drop. The nurse who rescued me from the helicopter stays by my side. An attractive, middle-aged woman with long blond hair pulled back in a ponytail, she is an angel, attending to my every need, never leaving my side. As she watches me cry and mumble to myself, she stands, stoic, smiling down at me with her comforting blue eyes. Her hands are soft and warm against my cool body, and she never breaks the contact. She is not a woman of many words, but her endless attention and loyal demeanor keep me calm. Under her steady gaze, I face the thought of the manner in which I will die.

Thrashing about and screaming is not the way I will leave this planet. No, not me. I will leave with courage, calmly and quietly. I know my passing will release me from pain, leaving my family to suffer the terrible consequences. I will my eyes to close, trying to calm my mind, but intermittent flashes of the attack break into the white space I try to find for myself. My body involuntarily flinches, and I can feel blood erupting from my wounds. Each time I open my eyes to escape the visions, I find myself fighting to live.

My right kneecap throbs. I had forgotten about that. I move to grab it and the nurse stops me. "What did he do to your poor knee?" she cries.

None of the doctors has noticed this contusion; the nurse's dismayed question rivets their attention to it. Everyone looks and demands to know what the attacker had done to me to cause this injury. I am amazed at everyone's concern.

"Nothing to do with...him," I whisper.

They are hovering over me so solicitously, so concerned about what happened, I push myself to explain as they examine my knee.

"I went biking before work this morning...no, yesterday morning," I say, trying to raise my voice so they can easily hear. "I usually do 10 miles. I rounded a corner and a car came from nowhere and clipped me...I tumbled over and landed flat on my knee. The guy left the scene....My bike was so smashed I had to limp home with my broken bike."

Their murmurs of sympathy are like a balm. They spend a few seconds feeling around the knee, bending my leg back and forth, then return their concentration to my other injuries.

I think about the accident. My new glasses flew off my face to rest precariously on the edge of a nearby storm sewer. I was so happy they hadn't fallen in, because I am blind without them.

"I didn't break my glasses, though," I say, as though the trauma team were reading my thoughts. "My lucky day, I told everyone. Then tonight...no, last night...this morning...when he attacked me"—I draw a long, rasping breath, a half-sob—"he took them from me and broke them in half."

The room is silent as they stare down at me. My angel nurse blinks rapidly, as though she is trying to keep back tears. A few moments later she bends toward me. "It's time, Donna.

Time to move you to surgery." As she begins to wheel my gurney out of the trauma room toward surgery, I felt an emptiness in my stomach. My heart aches for my family. *If I die, who will explain what really happened?* I wonder. Tears run from my eyes to my ears. I remember the first time my mom left me at school, and I thought I would never see her again. Now, today, we might truly be separated forever.

I am sailing through the dreary, cold corridor and I lift my head, aching to see someone I know. No familiar face is there as they wheel my gurney behind the closed doors of the surgery suite. Quickly I am lifted onto a cold, metal table. Warm blankets are gently put over my chilled body. Dr. Kessell, the attending trauma surgeon who is on call tonight, is fully gowned and standing next to my table. Dr. Karmi, who has been called in to repair my kidney, is also ready. They will operate on me simultaneously. The anesthesiologist, Dr. Thomas, walks over. I cannot see his mouth behind his mask, but I know he is smiling, for his cheeks are raised and his eyes are squinty.

"I'm going to insert some medicine into your IV, Donna," Dr. Thomas says. "It will make you sleepy."

"Wait," I say. "First I want to thank you all for everything you've done for me. If it doesn't work out for me, please know I am grateful."

"You, young lady, are going to be just fine," Dr. Thomas says firmly. "Now count backward from 100 for me."

"One hundred, 99, 98..."

2 Intensive Care

Baltimore City added its Shock Trauma Unit to the University Hospital, a training hospital, back in 1969. Ten years after the unit opened, the Baltimore City ambulance service abandoned its nearest-hospital policy, giving trauma patients a direct route to one of four designated centers. The most serious were automatically taken to Shock Trauma, University Hospital. That recent policy change undoubtedly saved my life.

I awoke in Shock Trauma's Intensive Care Unit, which had eight meticulously stocked cubicles for the most serious trauma patients. Each cubicle, indistinguishable from the others and separated only by white cloth curtains, included an electronic bed, heart monitor, respiration appliances, suction apparatus, tray table and two visitor chairs. Trauma patients require a full-time, one-on-one nurse around the clock. Crash carts, x-ray machines, backup generators and a portable CAT scan machine lined the outside hall of the unit for quick access.

My mother and sister walked slowly into ICU anticipating the worst. My mother, born and raised in Trieste, Italy, had come to America after marrying my father, and she dedicated her life to her children. She was a hard worker who struggled to learn the English language and customs, knowing she would be learning right alongside her kids. Raised poor, she never finished grade school, but she vowed to God her children would have better opportunities, especially a good education. And she kept that vow. In 1953 she lost a three-day-old daughter; now she faced the death of another child.

Mom and Debbie's heads turned side to side as they observed other trauma patients. Stopping short before approaching my bed (the last one on the right), they wiped their tearful eyes, painted plastic smiles on their faces and pulled the curtain back with a loud screech. My eyes flew open and were immediately full of tears in response to the bright fluorescent lights above me. I squinted at the two blurred figures before me. The mechanical respirator, a large tube inserted through my mouth and into my lungs, prevented me from speaking. The figures came closer and my vision cleared.

Dark circles were visible under my mother's eyes as she leaned down and kissed my forehead. She was cautious, not wanting to disturb the many tubes that were affixed one way or another to my body. The aroma of my mother's perfume washed over me, even after she turned away, overwhelmed with emotion. She didn't want me to see her tears, but the sound of her soft sobbing kept me alert and unable to fall back to sleep.

I was elated to see my mom and sis. For a second I felt everything was going to be all right, now that they were here. The tube in my throat, pushing air into my lungs, was huge, and I was extremely conscious of it, knowing it was ballooning my lungs, forcing them to do their job. My racing thoughts were jumbled. I just wanted to go to sleep and never wake up. I didn't want to deal with anything that was happening.

Yet even with all the pain medication dripping into my veins, I remained acutely alert to my mother's and sister's presence. It occurred to me they did not have to know what had happened to me. I knew I had been injured. I knew I had been raped. It would be my secret from everyone.

My mother continued to look away as Debbie, who is two years younger than I, pulled a chair next to my bed. Affectionately she placed her warm hand on my bruised and battered face, creating a moment of peace within me. As my head fell against her hand for support, I cried. Deb and I were close. When my parents divorced we got a place together. For more than two years we had been living in an apartment complex. After awhile, we had become more like friends than sisters. We did almost everything together—wore each other's clothes, shopped together, ate Sunday meals together and went to the same social functions. I remember the day we got approved for a new place, an apartment in a single-dwelling Cape Cod house in a quiet community. It was perfect for us, a basement apartment with all the amenities, including our very own washer and dryer, dishwasher, driveway and a spacious yard shaded with lots of trees.

As she sat with her hand against my face, I thought about how much I missed our house. I just wanted everything to go back to the way it had been. I hoped this was all a dream and I would suddenly wake up and everything would be the same. Their worried faces told me a different story. I knew I was in bad shape, and I hated having them seeing me in this condition.

"Sis," Deb said in a calm, soft voice, "the person who did this to you hasn't been caught. Two detectives are in the other room with Dad, Barb, Walt and Glenn. They have been talking to us all morning, hoping we could help them. They need our help. Your doctor gave us permission to come in for just a few minutes to see if you can help us. I know this will be hard, but we have to catch the son-of-a-bitch who did this to you. When I ask you a question, I need you to answer by blinking your eyes once for yes and twice for no. Okay?" She looked over toward Mom, who had turned back to face us.

When I nodded yes, the nasogastric tube slipped and scrapped painfully against my raw nasal lining, causing my right eye to tear.

"Don't try to nod," Debbie said. "Just blink once for yes. Did the guy who hurt you live around us?" she asked, her voice crackling with weariness.

I blinked once.

Deb smiled as she leaned closer toward me. "Do I know him?"

I blinked once, glancing at my mother from the corner of my eye.

"Did he hang around our old neighborhood with Billy and those guys?"

Ferndale Avenue, a linear road lined with decade-old residential tract houses, was commonly used by the community for quick access to the 7-Eleven store that was close to our house. Billy, a few years older, who lived at the other end of Ferndale Avenue, was not in our circle of friends. He and his buddies, all high school dropouts, would regularly walk by our house to congregate at the 7-Eleven store.

Suddenly our eyes locked, evoking an extrasensory transference between two determined minds to merge as one. I released my hand from her grip and with my index finger drew an invisible circle in the air around my temple. Debbie's eyes opened so wide her eyelids disappeared as she gave me a look of instant recognition. Her soft demeanor instantly transformed to fury.

"Kenny!" she said. I had not recalled his name until that moment, but hearing it caused such a fast-forward replay of my attack my body exploded in a violent convulsion.

3 Trauma Unit Two

One week to the day of my admission to the hospital at death's door, I was ready to be moved from Trauma Unit One, or ICU, as most people would call it. Trauma Unit One was a room with eight beds monitored 24 hours a day, with a private nurse for each bed. The Trauma Unit Two was a long hallway, up one floor, with approximately 10 semi-private rooms and one nurses' station. The unit had only one bed available, and that's where they put me. All the other rooms were occupied by severe trauma patients.

They tucked me into my bed and brought all my stuff. The curtain between me and the other bed was pulled closed, so I didn't know who was on the other side, nor did I think about it. In Trauma Unit One, I didn't feel the need or want to know who was next to me. I was just too sick. As I lay getting comfortable with my new surroundings, I began to unpack my valuables and toiletries into the tray table. Finally settled and needing rest from all that work, I lay back on my pillow. Covered in clean sheets and a warm, white blanket, I awaited my pain medication. The nurses so far had been excellent at giving it in a timely manner.

As I closed my eyes, feeling very comfortable, I heard a ruckus coming from the bed beside me. The curtain was closed between the beds, and I couldn't see through to the other side. I didn't pay much attention to it other than the fact that any noise startled me. Suddenly the curtain was pulled back. I opened my eyes to see a man with a shaved head, wearing nothing but scrub pants, walking past my bed and out the door. He didn't acknowledge me, but his presence alone scared the living hell out of me. The man was evil-looking, frightening and quiet. I sat straight up in bed and immediately rang for the nurse. The nurse came quickly.

"I can't stay in here with that man in the next bed," I said nervously.

"Now, now." She looked at me as though I were a little girl as she tried to tuck me back in bed. "You'll be fine. He's harmless."

"I'm not a child," I spat out. "I cannot stay in the same room with that man."

"It will be all right," she insisted. "That poor man wouldn't hurt a fly."

My lips were trembling and I struggled not to cry. "I want to speak to the head nurse," I said.

"Very well," the nurse said as she turned and walked out.

As I waited for the head nurse to come, I gathered all my belongings I had so neatly put away. They were all around me in the bed as I sat waiting to be moved.

The head nurse arrived, but she couldn't comprehend my fears. She, too, stated everything would be all right. Soon the hospital psychiatrist came walking in. He was a middle-aged, chubby man wearing a white coat with "Psychiatrist" stitched on it. He wanted me moved to the psychiatric ward. I couldn't believe my ears. He had not taken one second to talk to me in private to evaluate my concerns. I could only surmise he had read my chart and had made his determination from that. I was outraged. I thought for certain he would be the one to understand, but I was wrong. All these people, with all their experience, had no clue about what was happening. They weren't listening to me, which got me so angry I vomited.

All the nurses on duty were at my door, watching, as I got up from my bed, pulled my IV tree behind me, held my NG (nasal gastric) tube and suction container, and lurched into the hall. They were also watching as I collapsed in the middle of the hallway. Everyone was looking at me as if I were crazy. They knew the circumstances of my hospitalization, but they couldn't or wouldn't acknowledge what I needed. They just stood there looking at me.

Lying in that hallway made me look and feel like a deranged person, but I didn't care. I knew my feelings were perfectly normal, given the circumstances. This was not a game I was playing. The staff and the psychiatrist should have realized it had been just one week to the day that I was brutally attacked and almost killed. I just had surgery for God's sake! My scar ran straight across my belly from one side to the other, side to side, 20 inches long. With more than 70 stitches still intact, I could not stand erect. So there I lay, curled up on the floor. I was in the care of caregivers who would rather see me lying on this floor than attend to my emotional and physical needs. It seemed as though all these people standing above me were more concerned with how this looked than with taking care of the problem, which was obvious to me: I was scared out of my mind. Their inattentiveness made for more difficulties, since it riled up the other patients who could hear but were unable to get out of their beds to see what was going on. I knew I couldn't stand, so I remained on the floor. I needed a chair, but no one brought me one. They tried to pick me up and put me back in my room, but I fought them off.

"Call my mother!" I yelled. "Tell my mother to come get me, because I'm leaving if I have to stay in that room. There's no way I will room with that scary-looking man!" As I watched one of the nurses depart to make the phone call, I was seething. *Why can't anyone understand?* my mind screamed. *My God, all that I have been through. Is this a nightmare?*

I was hurting badly, and I continued to vomit in the hallway. The psychiatrist wanted to give me a sedative, but I refused. They were not going to pull that trick on me, putting me to sleep and then putting me back in that room. It was them against me. That's what it came down to. I was going to hold my ground 'til my mother got there. I was so scared as I lay there, looking up at them, registering the furious faces they were making at me. They wanted so much to take me away and put me in a locked ward. But I wasn't crazy. Why couldn't they understand? I was perfectly sane. I, just one week ago, survived against all odds to live, and now I was being treated like a crazy person. *What is wrong with these people?*

As soon as my mother got the phone call, she sped out the door and rushed to the hospital. She ran to my side.

"What's going on, Donna?" she asked. "Why are you out here?"

I told her what had happened.

"She has to have another room," Mom said.

The psychiatrist sidled up to her. "Your daughter is obviously disturbed," he said. "I'd like to move her to the psychiatric ward."

My mother got hot—really hot. She called for Dr. Karmi. He wasn't on duty, but the nurses beeped him and he called back. He couldn't believe what they had put me through, and he immediately told the staff to find me another bed with a female roommate. As quickly as the nurses were told, a bed was available. I will never understand why they put me through that ordeal. I can only suspect it was their lack of training with rape victims.

For the rest of my stay, I was comfortable in a semi-private room with a female roommate. One more ordeal was behind me.

Home, Sweet Home

"Is this the day?" I asked Dr. Karmi.

"No, not today. Maybe tomorrow."

Each morning I would wait for the doctor to get to me as he made his rounds.

"Is this the day?"

"Yes, Donna, this is the day."

"What? What did you say?"

The doctor laughed. "This is the day, Donna. You can go home today."

"Why today?" I asked.

He laughed again. "All those other days you wanted to know why not. Now today you want to know why." Dr. Karmi took my hand. "As much as I would like to keep you here, we need the bed. I still wouldn't let you go if I hadn't talked to your family this week about your care and been satisfied they're up to the task. I believe they understand what is involved and they are capable of caring for you and your urostomy bag."

The urostomy bag was a pouch glued to my left hip right above my buttocks. Its purpose was to detour urine out of my body, bypassing the damaged portion of my kidney and ureter, allowing them to heal. The bag would fill and I would measure its volume with what I drank that particular day. Because of its location behind me and on my left side, I would not be able to change it myself when it collapsed after a few days and began to leak. The doctor was now convinced my family could handle it.

"See you in three weeks, Donna," Dr. Karmi said as he walked out of the room.

I picked up the phone and dialed. "Mom! Come get me! I'm coming home!"

After 30 days in the hospital, I was going home! I sat on the bed, waiting for the results of final tests that would prove me ready for discharge. Before the final okay came through, I showered and dressed, so I was ready to go when Mom and Debbie came walking into my room. Their wide smiles matched mine. I was finally able to join the outside world. My last thoughts of the outside was the night of my attack, and I wanted to replace those awful visions with happier events. They helped me pack my suitcase with the cards and gifts so many people had sent to me. I had flowers, teddy bears, buttons, vases and lots of other special gifts I wanted to keep. Mom and Debbie had to figure out how to get them all to the car. I was still so weak I couldn't handle anything. Because of hospital protocol I was put in a wheelchair. My quick-thinking sister decided to pile everything they couldn't carry onto my lap. I laughed.

As I was being pushed down the long trauma corridor, all my nurses and a few doctors watched in silence as I approached. I felt tears come to my eyes, because I had become so attached to many of them. I remember one nurse who brought me a beer one night when I was watching a football game on television. I will never forget that. Another nurse came in off duty to give me a back rub, something I really enjoyed and needed after lying in bed all day. I remembered the many trauma patients that I would be leaving behind.

The 16-year-old who was shot in the back by her boyfriend. The young man in his thirties who was paralyzed because of a car accident. The 18-year-old beauty who was shot while she and her friends played around with a shotgun. She was paralyzed from her waist down. She and I became so close we would wash each other's hair and play cards, when both of us felt up to it. The nurses swore we were like sisters. I knew I would miss her the most. The last words she spoke to me were, "Donna, I promise you, I will walk again." And I believed her.

The one person who stuck out in my mind as I was leaving was the man they put me with in the semi-private room after releasing me from the Trauma Unit One. Now that I was leaving the hospital, I felt bad for him. I had discovered that he had cracked his skull in a hard fall on concrete, suffering brain damage. The surgery he needed required them to shave his head. He couldn't speak. I would see him walk up and down the halls when I was in bed at night. He still scared me, even after I knew what had happened to him. I don't think he ever realized what took place that night; I hope not. I knew and my mom knew and my doctor knew it had nothing to do with him. The problem was he was a guy, and he looked crazy.

Time had changed the attitudes of those nurses from "Are you happy now that you got your way?" to hugging and kissing me when I left. That early incident had been traumatic and uncalled for, and I can only pray it left a lesson for the future. I learned people can never truly understand something unless they've gone through it themselves. All I ask of others is that they simply learn to listen to all victims. This incident left me very sad, because the Shock Trauma Unit was for much more than head injuries, car accidents, bullet wounds and swimming accidents. Make way for the rape victims! I was obviously their first rape victim, and they didn't know how to handle me.

My injuries were physical, as were those of all the other trauma patients, but it was my emotions that crippled me more than anything else. The staff was trained only to handle the physical side. My nightmares, my screams and my fear of men were never understood or talked about. The psychiatrist was worthless. He was as bad as the staff that night, feeding into the minds of the staff members that I was crazy. Because of his title, everyone went along with him. He later tried to get me to come to his office for therapy, but his credibility had been irreparably damaged with me. He was a man, for one; for two, he wasn't about to get me alone with him in his office; and for three, his bedside manner was reprehensible.

As we exited through the front door of the hospital, I took a deep breath of the outside air. It was a glorious September day. Debbie went to get the car and my mom looked at me as if to say, *You made it, kid!* My look said to her, *I'm alive and I'm outside!*

People were everywhere. The hospital entrance had a circular sitting area made of concrete steps where many gathered for lunch and smoking. Each time I heard someone walking up behind me I jumped up from my chair, dropping my precious presents and causing me much pain. I finally asked Mom to stand behind me so no one would startle me anymore. She wasn't too sure what all that meant, but she did as I asked.

The ride home was quiet. There were a few comments about when the leaves might begin to turn. My mom had never known the right thing to say in any situation and this day was no exception, but I had learned to accept this about her. As for Debbie, she was concentrating on her driving, maneuvering the car as if she had just gotten her license, moving slowly and cautiously. I finally told her to step on it.

She was so nervous, trying not to make any sudden moves that would hurt me. It was a 30-minute ride to my house, and I enjoyed being outside and safe in their care.

We made the turn into the driveway and I could see a few cars. Then I saw my old Nova, Betsy. She was as rusty as I left her just 30 days earlier. Quickly, without warning, I flashed back to the night of the kidnaping, remembering that he, too, had a Nova, but his was blue. I began to cry, then struggled to put it out of my mind. There were people waiting, some inside the house, others coming toward the car as Debbie pulled to a stop. I didn't want to greet them with tears.

When we walked into the house, a cacophony of voices filled my ears. A handful of close friends and my sisters and brothers were present, and they attempted to hug me, but I rejected their affection. I was not yet ready for anyone to touch me. I asked Debbie to walk me through the house so I could see for myself that no one was lurking around that might scare me. I was a different person from the one they had known before. I was weak and vulnerable. I couldn't explain it to them, but it was obvious as they stood their distance, waiting for me to make the move. I just wanted to go to bed. They were all healthy and happy, ready to socialize; but I wanted to be alone. For their benefit I lay on the couch so, individually, one after another they would come sit by me and console me. *What do I say to these people?* I had so much going through my head, I could not think of how to hold a conversation.

When they would leave me alone for a few minutes, I would peer into the kitchen where they were gathered. Intermittently I flashed back to the good ol' days, the days when I would have been right in there with a beer in my hand, sharing stories and making plans to do such and such. But now I was alone in my own terror and loneliness.

Finally, the evening was over. Days passed, and my health was terrible—fevers, problems with my urostomy bag leaking, vomiting and sleeplessness. Debbie had to return to work, leaving me home to fend off the private demons that lurked around the house. Any small noise forced me under my bed or into my closet. I had no one to call or ask over. Everyone worked. I believed in my heart my loved ones loved me and wanted to help me, but they had no clue. Neither did I. I was scared, in pain and lost in a new world of violence and terror.

When the mailman came, the sound of the mailbox lid closing caused me to hide. Even though this happened every day except Sunday, it still never clicked in my mind it was the mailman. I never shared these feelings with anyone because they sounded so ridiculous. I would often peek through the front curtains that I kept closed to make sure no one was watching me. I was scared out of my mind. I couldn't watch television or listen to the radio as I could in the hospital, but I knew the silence was not good for me. The phone would ring, but I refused to pick it up. Even though I knew my sister wanted to call to see how I was doing, I was too afraid it was Kenneth Morgan trying to locate me. He was constantly around me.

My half brother, Walter, who is 12 years older than I, came to watch over me for a few days. He stayed overnight and cooked for me, really being a great brother. One day I was locked in my bedroom—something I did a lot—and Walter knocked on my door. "Donna, Kenny is here to see you," he called softly.

All hell broke loose. I thought for sure Kenneth Morgan had found his way to my house and was going to finish me off. "Walter!" I yelled. "Get that son-of-a-bitch out of this house! He is here to kill me. Get him out! Get him out! Get him out!" I repeated the demand over and over at the top of my voice.

Walter just kept saying, "It's just Kenny, Donna. He's not going to hurt you."

"I know only one Kenny," I shouted, "and he's the guy who hurt me!"

"Donna," Walter said, his mouth at the door, "this is one-legged Kenny, Debbie's friend."

I slid down on the floor, my back against my bed. I began to calm down slowly. There was a light knock at my door. "Hey, Donna, it's Kenny. You know, one of the good guys. I didn't mean to upset you. I'll come back another day. So sorry I upset you. I'll talk to you later."

Hearing his voice, I remembered. Kenny. The sweetest guy in the whole world. The guy I wanted my sister to marry. He was the guy we called one-legged Kenny because he had lost his leg in a motorcycle accident a few years back. Still, I didn't move. I heard him leave.

As soon as Debbie came home from work I could hear her and Walter talking about what happened. She started yelling. "Don't you know the guy who hurt Donna was named Kenny? No wonder she had a fit." Walter left, confused, and never volunteered his time with me again. The poor guy had never been subject to anything like this before and he later told me, "I didn't understand."

5 Therapy Session

On a Monday morning in October I lay in bed, thinking of the promise I had made to Debbie. She was taking me to the Rape Crisis Center that day, and I had promised her I wouldn't cancel. I wasn't looking forward to it...dreading it, in fact, but I had to do something. It was just that I had met Ina Nortan, the director of the center, while I was in the hospital, and I didn't care for her. How could she help me if I didn't like her?

I had been lying in my hospital bed in the Shock Trauma Step Down Unit when she dropped in, unannounced. Her long, curly, black hair didn't seem to fit her cool demeanor when she walked into my room, saying a family member had asked her to stop in. She was sloppily dressed, and I wondered what kind of therapist didn't care any more than this for her appearance. Actually, I wasn't very nice to her at all. I blamed it on the medication, but I truly didn't make an effort. She had stayed only a few moments, then said goodbye, leaving her business card on my side table.

I later learned that her schedule had been hectic that day, and she was squeezing in the visit to me between other commitments. That resolved the issue of the way she was dressed.

But now I thought about facing her again. Not only did I dread the therapy session, of which I had no understanding, I felt embarrassed about the way I had behaved at our first meeting.

Reluctantly I got myself ready that morning, and much more quickly than I wished, Debbie pulled up in the center parking lot. The autumn colors may have been brilliant along the road that day; the sky was probably bright blue, without a cloud in sight. I did not notice.

"Rape Crisis Center," read the sign on the door. I turned the knob and walked in. Debbie followed behind. When the heavy wooden door snapped closed, I jumped, thinking someone had come in behind us. I grabbed my sister's arm for comfort and protection.

Ina walked in from an adjoining room. "Hello, Donna. I'm glad you're here."

I raised my eyes from the gray carpet, feeling the heat in my cheeks. "Thank you," I said, making myself look her in the eye. "This is my sister, Debbie. She'll wait for me."

"It's a pleasure to meet you, Debbie....Well, I guess we should get started." Ina pointed toward the room she had just exited.

"Okay," I said with a sigh. "I guess I'm ready." I released my firm hold on my sister and walked slowly toward the other room.

"I'll be right here when you come out," Debbie assured me as she sat down on a leather couch. "I'm right here. Don't forget that."

Ina and I walked into a spacious but cluttered room. Toys and construction paper with children's drawings were strewn on the furniture and floor. As Ina cleared off a cloth chair for me, she apologized for the mess. "This room is used for daycare on the weekends," she said with a smile. "I guess you could call it multi-purpose....Please! Won't you sit down?"

I sat as directed. Ina retrieved another chair from the middle of the daycare paraphernalia and pulled it facing mine. Simultaneously, we crossed our legs, then burst out laughing. The warm, bubbling sound thawed the chilled atmosphere.

Ina's friendly smile replaced the look of cool professionalism I noticed when we first met. Even so, she sat erect, careful not to invade my space. "Donna, I, too, was a victim of a violent crime. Although the particulars of the assault against me were not as severe as yours, I still carry the guilt and emotional trauma associated with my attack."

In stunned silence, I listened as she bared her soul to me. This was certainly not the way I envisioned the therapy session would begin.

"The man entered my small apartment while I was taking a bath," she said, her eyes never leaving mine. "Before I knew anyone had entered my home, he was in the bathroom, pulling me from the bathtub and gagging me." She shook her head. "The worst part was that my two little children were sleeping in the next room. I couldn't scream. It would have terrified them, and if they had come into the room, they would have been in danger. So I swallowed the screams that were ripping through my mind as he dragged me to my bedroom." Ina closed her eyes briefly, remembering. "He stayed all night long, holding me locked in his arms, continually raping me. When dawn broke, he nonchalantly left through the front door....He was never apprehended."

My first reaction was to want to reach out and embrace her. Instead, I shut down, folding my arms tightly around my small torso, as if to protect myself from hearing any more. My body language spoke louder than any words. My response angered me. This is who I had become, a person who could not offer consolation to another.

I thought back to the day I returned home from the hospital, with my family standing, waiting, as I got out of the car.

There I was, wearing a urostomy bag and still hunched over from my surgery, wishing mightily I could fend them off. They came toward me like a swarm of bees greeting their queen, but as they embraced me, I stood as stiff as a Buckingham Palace guard. These compassionate people were my family. They had not given up hope that one day I would come home, and now their hopes had come to pass. I was there. But I had offered nothing but my presence.

Ina pulled her chair closer to mine, suddenly encroaching on my protective space. As she leaned forward, I felt threatened. Beads of sweat began to form on my forehead and my moist hands slid down my bare arms, as I gripped them tightly. A sudden metamorphosis occurred. Instead of a warm human, I became a cold manikin. My catatonic condition was read immediately by Ina, and she instantly retreated.

Cautiously she asked, "Donna, do you want to talk about what you are feeling right now?"

Slowly I could feel my protective armor peeling off in sections, releasing the tightness in my muscles and causing my limbs to relax. I moved my eyes around the room to reorient myself. Even though I was relaxing, I was still guarded. "What am I feeling? Good question, Ina. I don't feel safe here."

I glanced at the door. "The only safe feeling I have right now is in the knowledge that my sister is in the other room, guarding the door against potential attackers. I know it sounds silly, but I am so frightened of everything and everybody. Even you! There is a small part of my brain that believes you are here to help me, but still I am unsure of your intentions. I…I've lost my train of thought…I'm sorry." I lowered my chin to my chest, but I could still see Ina.

She perched forward again in her chair, putting her hands together in a praying manner. "The purpose of our meeting is to help you cope with these feelings. I can guarantee you this is a safe place. Neither I nor anyone else will hurt you here."

A flash of memory, like a snapshot, streaked across my mind. My attacker had said words to that effect.

"You've suffered a tremendous amount of trauma, both physically and mentally," Ina continued. "From what your family has told me, you've shut them out. It's been what? Two months since your attack?"

"Yes, that's correct. August third, to be exact." I cleared my throat. "Ironically, I wasn't even scheduled to work that night. My normal schedule was Saturday through Wednesday. Diana, the designated trainer for new managers and a very sweet person, called and asked if I would work Thursday because the clerk called in sick. Without hesitation, I told her it would be fine. She treated me well, and every opportunity I had to return the favor, I would. She was so very fair in her decisions. She offered me the weekend off for filling in that day, and her generosity was welcomed, since I had plans to take my mother to her first Italian Festival on Sunday at Baltimore's Inner Harbor."

Everyone knew about the place. Baltimore City had built it in 1980—two bi-level, glass-enclosed twin pavilions, located on the water's edge of the inner harbor. Comprising eight ethnic restaurants, prestigious novelty shops and cafés with outdoor seating overlooking the harbor, Baltimore Harbor hosted several hundred special events annually, from ethnic festivals, famed street performers and Santa's Place at Christmastime.

"That was a very nice thing you were doing for your mother," Ina commented, sitting back in her chair in a more comfortable position.

"I think I was more excited about taking my mother than she was about my taking her. As a kid, I always wanted to do nice things for her, but there was so much chaos in my house, I never did. I'm glad I'm here to have a second chance. I remember the day I was allowed to get out of my bed at the hospital. Balancing myself with my IV pole, I walked over to a window that faced the Harbor and…"

Ina passed me a tissue as tears began to roll down my face.

"What did you mean when you said there was a lot of chaos in your house?" Ina asked with interest.

"My father is an angry alcoholic," I replied. "He would come home late at night, waking my mother and us kids from a deep sleep. He would accuse her of being unfaithful. His loud yelling would even wake our neighbors, bringing them out of their homes. My mother, not a passive woman, would explode like a firecracker, causing an already bad situation to get worse. Before you knew it, they would be physically abusing each other and breaking furniture. The neighbors would call the police and my father would go to jail. These fights really upset my two sisters and me. We would sit at the top of the stairs huddling together. When things quieted down we retreated to our rooms."

I wiped a stray tear from my cheek. "Our parents never asked how these altercations made us feel," I continued. "That is one thing about my parents: they never talked about feelings. My father would come home the next morning a different person, begging my mother for forgiveness. He is a nice man when he isn't drinking. My mother would stay mad for a few days, then take him back. Their reunion brought security back to the house." I looked down at my hands, feeling vaguely guilty for divulging the family secret.

"How old were you when this would happen?" Ina asked.

"First let me say, I love my parents," I replied. "They had problems, and that's how they dealt with them. My parents divorced a few years ago.…I guess, if anything really bothered me, above all, it was the fact my mother would try to reason with him when he was drunk. To answer your question, I was around eight or ten years old."

"What kind of relationship do you have with your father?" she asked.

"If you're asking about my attack, my father has never talked about it with me! I am aware of a phone call my father received the morning after my attack, by someone my *attacker* confided in. I don't know what was said, but to date my father has never talked to me about it. That's what kind of relationship we have. I can't help but feel he blames me for what happened!"

"Donna, did you know your attacker?" Ina pressed.

"Well...I didn't make him do this to me!" I screamed. "He's sick! Just because I was nice to him when he came into my store doesn't mean I made this happen!" I was sobbing, and tears ran in streams from my bulging eyes.

"Donna, can you hear me?" Ina asked. "Listen, please! I know you didn't do anything wrong that night. What happened to you had nothing to do with anything you said or did. Perpetrators, no matter whether they know their victim, have made up their minds what their intent is way before the victim is confronted." Ina spoke with fervor, but her words were small consolation at that moment.

"Ina, can I go home now? I'm so exhausted."

"I would like you to come back. I want to help you very much. May I say I think you are the most courageous person I have ever met. I know, by working together, we can uncover these inner feelings and make good use of them. Donna, you are a survivor. I know that is why you are here today. You have lived through something most don't survive. You value your life enough to have survived this horrendous attack. I would like you to come see me twice a week. Can you come back on Thursday?" She grabbed her schedule book.

"I'll need to check with my sister to see if she can bring me," I began, then made a decision in midsentence. "I...uh...never mind. Yes, I will come back."

The days passed quickly as I anticipated my next session. Locked in my bedroom, leaving only to go to the bathroom or get something to eat, I felt like a prisoner. I would look outside my window, watching cars speed by and people walking their dogs. When the mailman would come to drop the mail in the door slot, I would hide.

I couldn't watch TV or listen to music because it made too much noise. I needed to hear everything that was going on. Even the phone ringing became a nuisance because it was so loud. I would attempt to read the many magazines I had been given in the hospital only to be interrupted by the sound of the refrigerator kicking on or a car turning around in the driveway. The smallest sound startled me into a panic attack.

I sat in the same chair as at my first session. Ina looked quite lovely this day. Her long, black, curly hair fell over her shoulders. She was dressed in a beautiful, bright green, two-piece suit with an angel pinned to her lapel. I was wearing sneakers, a tee shirt and size-eight blue jeans, baggy now, that used to fit.

"I'm glad you came back. How are you today, Donna?" Ina asked.

"I'm fine." To myself, I chuckled, thinking of the acronym a friend told me once: F.I.N.E.—Fucked up. Insecure. Neurotic. And Emotional. I thought it apt, but I didn't mention it. Instead, I commented, "I like your outfit."

"Thank you," she replied. "Since our last session I've been thinking about you a lot. I want our sessions to go at your pace. If you feel uncomfortable talking about something, I need you to tell me so I can understand." She waited for my nod of comprehension, then continued. "You told me at your last session you weren't supposed to be working the night of your attack. When did you start working at the convenience store?"

"After my graduation from high school, my mother got me a job at a box factory where she had worked for many years. It paid good money and the hours were great. I was hired to work in the printing department, a section built specifically within the confines of the warehouse, which produced specialty printing for large retail corporations like Macy's, J.C. Penney, Dillard's, Hecht's and Sears. My natural ability and coordination skills preempted the usual training period. Within only a few days I was given my own machine and was kicking out orders. I enjoyed this so much I never wanted to take a break or eat lunch. But because it upset my peers, and because it broke the union rules, I conformed."

Ina nodded her understanding.

"After five years, though, things changed. My mother, who worked in one of the hardest departments, suddenly developed back problems, forcing her to transfer to my department. Because I was the least senior person, I got bumped. My mother moved in and I moved out. My hours changed to nights, and my new position was so unexciting and tedious I became very unhappy. So unhappy, I quit!" Across my mind flashed a picture of the night I walked off the line and right out the door.

"Did it make you angry your mom did this to you?" Ina asked curiously.

"I don't react well to change, but in hindsight I know there was meaning behind it. I subconsciously knew I didn't want to spend my life working in a factory. I wanted to go to college and make something of myself. I believe things happen for a reason. When all this happened, it forced me to make a change. Most important was the fact that my mother was able to continue to work. She had gotten me the job, and

I owed it to her to reciprocate....Um, may I have a glass of water, please?"

After taking a sip of the water Ina gave me, I continued. "A rolling stone gathers no moss. That's me! I decided to go to college, and the minute my feet landed on campus, I knew I belonged there. I stopped students for directions to admissions, and soon I was speaking to a counselor." My adrenalin rushed as I spoke of my goals and aspirations to Ina, and I could feel a smile light up my face. I have never had the opportunity to share this with anyone, and it felt good.

"Determined and excited after leaving the college campus, I drove around my hometown of Glen Burnie filling out job applications at various retail businesses. When I stopped to get a cheeseburger, I noticed a convenience store district office behind McDonald's in the residential neighborhood there. I walked over and filled out an application. I was immediately interviewed by the district manager and hired. I was told a brand new store was opening in the Early Heights area and they needed someone. All the pieces of my puzzled life were coming together. I could go to college during the day and work at night. Ina, I can't begin to tell you how happy I was that day."

Ina reacted instantly. "That story tells who you really are. Your strong-minded determination and motivation are great gifts. You quit a secure job after five years, confident of finding another. You went to the community college with great expectations of achieving a long-range goal. Most people wouldn't have done what you did. You put your mind to it and took the risk."

"Gee, I've never looked at it that way," I responded.

"When did you start your college courses?" Ina asked.

"I managed to squeeze in for the summer courses. Because of money—rather, lack of it!—I signed up for only two classes, English 101 and Psychology 101. Both were offered during the day. So, it worked out great for me."

"How did your parents react to your new job and going to college?" Ina queried.

"Well, my mother was glad I got another job so quickly. She made me a chocolate cake to celebrate. I never told my father, but I think he might have heard it from one of my sisters. It wasn't that important to me that he knew. He had remarried, and I didn't see him much. My future was never important to my father, anyway. When he came to the hospital to visit me after the attack, he was drunk. I haven't gotten over that. He would just stand over my bed, staring, reeking of alcohol and never saying a word. My mother would eventually tell him to leave." The control my father held over me seemed to pin me to my seat, and my head dropped forward. A long pause ensued, and I flashed back to the day of the attack.

Standing outside the convenience store…he comes up behind me…puts a knife against my throat…throws me into his car.

My body jerked with the memory and pain, and the jolt nearly lifted me from the chair.

"Where were you just now?" Ina probed.

"I think I've had enough today. Is it okay if I go home now?" I anxiously asked.

"Are you sure? I have plenty of time open for you if you want to continue." Ina's voice was full of sympathy.

"I'm tired now," I answered. "Also, I have a doctor's appointment tomorrow. They're supposed to remove my urostomy bag, and I'm kind of excited about that. This bag has been a complete nuisance. It leaks all the time. When it leaks my poor sister has to change it for me because I can't reach it to do it. Sometimes I have to wake her up early in the morning to do it. My sister has been so good, helping me with this and taking good care of me." I stood and picked up my jacket.

"Will you call me and tell me how it went?" Ina asked. "I'll be here in the office all day tomorrow....Let's go ahead and reschedule for Monday. Same time okay with you?"

"That works out great for my sister," I replied. "This same time every Monday and Thursday, right? Because my sister got permission from her boss indefinitely to bring me on these days and times." I was speaking quickly, and my mind was racing. *I think that's what Deb told me. God, my mind is so enmeshed with emotion, my short-term memory is shorting out.*

"Mondays and Thursdays, same time," Ina concurred. I'll see you Monday...and Donna, good luck with your doctor's appointment."

6 University Hospital

Anxious about returning to the hospital for my follow-up appointment, I skipped breakfast. My sister Barbara was taking time from her job to drive me there, and I was grateful. She came in, smiling and excited, to help me shower and dress. I didn't share with her the bad feeling I was having about the day, chalking it up under the list of negative thoughts that clouded my mind.

Over the past few days or so I had been feeling a dripping sensation inside my skin when I lay on my right side. I never said anything to anybody about it, trying to assure myself it was nothing to worry about. It probably had something to do with the urostomy bag. No sooner had we left the driveway than my fears began. I was now outside, vulnerable to the unknown.

Barbara put her hand on my lap. "Everything will be all right, Hon. We'll be back home in no time."

Trying to smile, I nodded. I believed her. My appointment was only to remove the urostomy bag, then…home, sweet home.

The ride to the hospital was uneventful as Barbara and I shared small talk. I felt at ease with her because no matter what, she was the older sister, always there to protect me. For the first time in months I was feeling intermittent positive thoughts about today, though they were not to be shared or said aloud. I thought of the new year. It was only October, but just for a few minutes, I felt once I got detached from this urostomy bag I would be free to look forward.

We entered Baltimore City's speed limit zone and then, as clear as day, there was University Hospital. An ancient English-style fort-like structure made of brownstone and brick, it stood in sharp contrast to other buildings on the impoverished streets around it. Its ambience, ironically, had been compromised by its accreditation as the first exclusive trauma facility in the state. Soon after the accreditation, volume demanded a concrete-block high-rise addition to the mother structure, encroaching on the historic status of the old building.

The many times I had come into the city to watch an Orioles game or eat at some of the great restaurants, I had never realized its beauty. Through my month-long hospitalization there, I always looked from the inside, out. Now as Barbara and I pulled into the parking lot, I really got a chance to admire the ancient building. What a magnificent edifice.

Immediately upon entering the newer part of the facility, the smell of iodine antiseptic pulled me back, and as I walked I experienced intermittent flashbacks of my initial admittance. Barbara, unaware of my visions, briskly walked up to the information desk and cordially requested directions to the outpatient Shock Trauma Clinic. To avoid confusion because of the hospital's many clinics, three- by five-inch index cards with maps to various destinations were on hand. Barbara was given a card with a detailed map to Shock Trauma.

As the elevator doors shut, I suddenly felt completely closed in. I couldn't breathe. Quickly taking in what was happening, Barbara grabbed my hand and said, "Hold on, kid!

We'll only be a minute." Her voice was nervous, but soothing.

Here I was having flashbacks and panic attacks, in the presence of everyone packed into the elevator. But I held them in tightly, afraid all these strangers would read my thoughts and feelings. At last the automatic doors opened into the isolated, dreary hallway I remembered so vividly. My perspiring hand slipped out of my sister's firm grip. All this walking was very hard for me, but I didn't want to complain. I had enough stuff going on that my sister needed to deal with. I left it alone.

Barbara grimaced as we passed the small, glass-enclosed waiting room designated for the families of Shock Trauma patients in surgery. It was the room in which she and my family had waited for hours until I was out of surgery, not knowing if I would make it. I could only imagine what a frightful, frightening day it had been for all of them. The room today was empty, as was the triage area next to it. Casually I looked into the trauma room, envisioning myself lying on that gurney with all the doctors and nurses around me trying to save my life. I remembered the rape kit test, especially when the nurse took a thin knife and cleaned under my bitten fingernails to gather evidence. I had endured this, not knowing anything about crime scenes or evidence, wondering why they were putting me through such torture at that point. Haunting memories clouded my mind as we continued walking down the long hallway.

A small red sign read, "Out Patient Shock Trauma Clinic." We walked in. Inside and to my left was the small waiting area. Exhausted from my long walk, I sat as my sister went to sign me in. While I waited for Barbara to return, I glanced around the small waiting room. Most of the patients were in wheelchairs and wearing halos to immobilize the spine. I wondered how they viewed me. I showed no visual scars, but underneath my well-groomed, mobile exterior, unseen by the naked eye, I, too, was paralyzed—paralyzed by terror, fearing everyone around me. Any quick motions or sounds wreaked havoc with my intellectual attempt to compose myself, exposing startle responses that were so intense at times my entire body would unexpectedly jolt.

My sister returned with a nurse and a wheelchair, for which I was grateful. They wheeled me to the radiology room and prepped me for an IVP—Intravenous Pyelogram. Anticipating this to be the last injection I would ever endure, I gladly welcomed the test. The dye solution was placed in a thick, long needle and inserted into a vein in my arm, causing an immediate warm sensation throughout my body. They then took intermittent x-rays of my kidney.

When I returned to the waiting room, Barbara greeted me with a cup of coffee and a piece of chocolate cake (my favorite) from the cafeteria. Just as I was about to take a big bite of cake, the nurse rushed over to tell me not to eat or drink anything 'til my test results were checked. My sister and I giggled softly.

We had waited only a few seconds after the nurse left when my urologist, Dr. Karmi, walked over toward me with my x-rays. He greeted us with his warm smile and asked us to follow him to his office. I gave my sister a puzzled look, then shrugged my shoulders and followed the doctor. Once inside his small office, he asked us to sit down.

"Donna, we have a problem," Dr. Karmi said, placing the x-rays on the fluorescent viewer. I could feel my chest tighten and my heart rate increase. I quickly looked at my sister, who came up behind me and put her hands on my shoulders.

"What's wrong, Dr. Karmi?" I asked, not really wanting to know the answer.

"Donna," he said, his Middle Eastern accent apparent even in the way he said my name, "we need to operate. Now. As you can see"—he pointed to the x-rays—"the repair we made to your ureter has detached, causing urine to leak into your belly. Have you eaten today?" He picked up the phone to call the OR as he waited for my reply.

"No, I haven't, but Dr. Karmi..." I stopped. He was already speaking into the phone.

In seconds the nurse came into the room with a wheelchair. Giving Barbara permission to follow, the nurse whisked me out of the room. I was rushed through the corridors like Mario Andretti. This must be serious. Maybe that dripping sensation I had felt was urine inside me. I've been told it was like poison in the system. Just the thought of another surgery was incomprehensible to me. I wasn't even healed from the first one...now, another. Fear began to build within me, and I kept looking back at Barbara for support, focusing on hearing her positive, soothing words as she struggled behind us, trying to keep up.

Suddenly we stopped and I was immediately placed in a room, disrobed, and put in a hospital gown. *What is going on!* My sister was not allowed in, nor was she able to say anything to me. Things were happening so fast, I couldn't think straight. The nurse had me lie on a metal gurney, placing my feet in stirrups. *Oh, my God, I am not comfortable with this.* The nurse covered my knees with a sheet.

Three doctors with surgical masks entered the room. No "Hello, how ya doin'"—nothing. I heard the door open again and another nurse came in. Here I was lying flat on my back in stirrups with three male doctors looking at me. A nurse stood on each side of me, each taking hold of one of my arms. I just looked up at them, wanting to know what in the world was going on. Again the door opened and Dr. Karmi came in, wearing surgical scrubs. Finally, someone I knew!

As he snapped rubber gloves onto his hands, he said, "Donna, this procedure will be very uncomfortable. Just hang in there, okay?"

I still didn't know what was going on. The other doctors were holding plastic bags with some kind of tubing of different lengths. They kept their eyes focused on Dr. Karmi, waiting for instruction. Without warning, an object entered my urethra, burning, feeling like a knife. I screamed with pain.

"Easy, Donna. Calm down, now. I need to get this catheter inside the bladder and up into your ureter so I can try to reconnect the two to stop the leaking. Unfortunately, I can only go by feel, which makes this very difficult....Donna, this may take some time. Just try to relax. Please! I know this is painful, but I am trying as hard as I possibly can to get this done. As I told you, the ureter has broken apart. Time is of the essence. You are losing so much urine into your body, and this procedure is very important to you. If we had a room in the OR, I would have you there and sedated, but unfortunately all the rooms are occupied and this is our only alternative."

Timing is everything, I thought, steeling myself to accept the pain.

Dr. Karmi continued to push the catheter through as he spoke, trying to calm me with his voice.

"Stop! It hurts! I can't take this!" I yelled. "Stop, please stop! You can't be serious to put me through all this pain without some kind of pain medication. I'm not a piece of meat. I'm a person. Please, stop! Barbara! Barbara, help me!" I screamed at the top of my lungs.

I was in pure agony. My stomach incision was burning with pain when I lifted my body off the table. There was no stopping this doctor. I tried gritting my teeth to stop myself from screaming, pumping my fists to endure the pain, but screaming helped the best, and by God, that is what I did. No one in the room seemed to be bothered by my cries.

Time after time the catheter would be pulled out of me and a new one inserted. Smaller ones, then larger ones, were tried over and over again. The pain was intense. The nurses standing on either side of me didn't say a word—they just watched—but I knew because they were female they were praying this would end.

"Just try to relax, Donna," Dr. Karmi said. "I can't work with you moving around."

"Give me something for pain, please!" I exclaimed in a moment of peace when they were switching off for new tubes.

"Donna, I can't give you anything now. As soon as we get this in we will be going to the operating room," Dr. Karmi said, looking at me.

"Okay. I'm okay," I said, gritting my teeth, waiting for the next onslaught. I had a really bad feeling there was no stopping him from completing this procedure.

It seemed like an eternity of profound pain as Dr. Karmi tried unsuccessfully to place the various sized catheters into my ureter. His determination was endless. Sweat beads formed on his forehead and rolled down his face. I could see him clearly over the sheet that had been placed over my knees. Without hesitation another bag was opened and another catheter was inserted.

"It's in!" Dr. Karmi declared, blowing out air, flipping off his surgical gloves and giving me a quick smile.

"But doctor, it still hurts. It's killing me," I protested as I pulled my legs from the stirrups.

"I have to leave you in the hands of these great nurses while I try to find an OR. The quicker I get one the quicker I can get you out of pain. Just hang in there." As he rushed out of the room he called over his shoulder, "I know you can do it."

The nurses pushed my gurney out of the room and into the hallway in front of the OR entrance. People were everywhere. The most important person was still waiting there for me: my sister. I was so happy to see her. She looked saddened for me, but I couldn't say anything to her. The discomfort of the catheter was so intense I could barely utter a word.

"I heard your screams," Barbara said softly in my ear. "Whatever they did to you in there was awful. I could hear your cries. I felt so bad for you with all you've been through. I so wish I could take this pain from you and let you rest." She continued to speak softly to me until a nurse interrupted.

"Donna, you'll have to stop wiggling around. You have to lie still, or you'll disturb the catheter's location."

Easy for you to say, I thought to myself. I motioned for my sister to lean down so I could tell her I couldn't take the pain anymore. It was hard for me to speak because with every breath my belly moved, sending a sharp, stabbing pain from my urethra to my kidney. I spoke to her in very short breaths, as if they were my last. I literally wanted to stop breathing to stop this horrific pain.

Awareness of people walking by me in the wide hallway forced me to soften my sobs. I must have lain there for an hour without any information from a nurse or doctor. At one point my sister felt so sorry for me, she started grabbing for anyone wearing a white jacket. But no one was willing to help.

I knew my pain threshold had been breached when my moaning became so loud it put me right where I didn't want to be: the center of attention. People stopped in their tracks to see what was going on with me. My sister would try to explain, but I didn't care anymore. For one quick instant I thought, *I should have just died that night.*

Panic-stricken by the long wait, the inattentiveness and my continued moaning and crying, Barbara pushed through the automatic doors of the operating room demanding someone's help. A young orderly in white scrubs came quickly to my side and told me I was next in line for surgery and Dr. Karmi was scrubbing up.

"Thank you," I said, gasping for air.

Seconds after he walked away, he returned and wheeled me in. My scrunched facial expression was all my sister saw before I disappeared behind the closed automatic doors. After a grueling three-hour surgery, I was taken to the only bed available...on the geriatric floor.

As was common, I had an NG tube and IV lines. I was not a happy camper. I was suffering with a lot of pain—a continuous, agonizing pain. Not until Dr. Karmi came in did I learn that he had removed one of my ribs to get around to make the repair. Bone pain is the worst pain imaginable. It felt as though I was lying on a metal basketball, no matter which way I turned. There was a constant, throbbing pain that was not eased by one of the best pain medications—morphine.

This pain, this surgery and the inconvenience of it all took their toll on my emotions. I was getting angrier by the minute. I tried—I really tried—to be a good patient, good sister and a good friend, but the pain turned me into a monster. I absolutely could not control my temper, no matter how much I tried.

Seven days later the NG tube came out, stitches from a long suture cut up my back were removed and the urostomy tube that had been a part of me for so long was pulled out. My kidney functions were back to normal and I was passing urine like everyone else. Dr. Karmi was a miracle worker.

Leaving the hospital, I thought of Ina Nortan, and how desperately I needed her. She had opened a part of me I was not willing to close again. I wanted to get better. I wanted to move on with my life. I knew the pain in my side would eventually go away over time, but the emotional pain was eating me alive. I was ready to talk. I needed to talk. I wanted to talk.

7 Guilt

Ina greeted me at the door. It was November, a month after our last meeting. I still looked the same, skinny, disheveled…and frightfully depressed. Ina quickly brought me into the therapy room. "Donna, did you drive yourself here?" she asked, pointing to the chair in which she wanted me to sit.

"If you must know, yes," I replied. "I'm so tired of relying on others. I feel this way: if something happens to me, so be it. I'm sick and tired of living like this. A caged animal. A trapped victim." I could feel the heat in my face as I made my declaration.

"Let's sit and talk," Ina suggested. "I'm so glad you decided to come back."

"Well, did you know I had to have surgery?"

"Yes, Debbie called and told me. I was going to come see you, but I wasn't sure if that was something you wanted."

"I had a very hard time with it, Ina, so it was better you didn't, although I could have used your wisdom. Nobody understands me—what I'm going through and all. I'm getting very close to dying inside. I can feel it. My world is dark and gloomy." *Why did I just say that? Am I looking for sympa-*

*thy, or what? I don't need her sympathy or anyone else's. It's my
life, so what? I don't need anyone.*

Ina broke into my thoughts. "Well, it sure sounds as though
we have lots of work to do. Let's begin with you telling me
what you are feeling today. I think that would be a good
place to start." She waited as I composed my answer.

I took a deep breath and slowly exhaled through my nose.
"Where do I begin? Today. How do I feel today? Hmmm…I'm
angry. I'm scared. I'm a worthless piece of shit. My life is
gone. I see no future. I can't stand waking every day to find
the quiet stench of life. I don't care about anything or anybody. I just want to fade away." I began to cry.

"I want to hear more," Ina said softly.

*Poor Ina, you have no idea what you are asking. I am so
angry I could just about say anything at any time, and it probably won't be so damn pleasant.* Again I took a deep breath.
"I'm 25 years old and I don't have a damn thing. One minute
I was fast-tracking up my ladder to success, and the next I
was fighting to stay alive. Before my attack I was going places,
meeting important people who now look at me like an injured animal. People think—and they are probably
right—once something like this happens to you, you are finished. To tell you the truth, I am finished. I'm maxed out. I
have always, since I can remember, wanted to be someone,
do something that would make people proud. Today, I am a
burden, a good-for-nothing parasite who feeds off others. Look
what I have become. That son-of-a-bitch, I hope he rots in
jail! He took my life away from me, and I am so God damned
angry. I wish…"

"You wish what?" Ina prompted.

*Yeah, repeat my last words. I know all about this therapy
shit. Well, if you want to know so much, you are going to hear it.*
I clenched my fists. "I wish I could get one minute with him."

"Tell me, Donna. What would you do?"

"You don't want to know what I would do. I'd take a gun and blow his damn balls off. That's what I would do. I would then hang him from the wall and let him bleed to death, just as he did to me. But he would not survive, because I am much smarter than he is. I would make damn sure he was dead before I left....He will rot there 'til he dies. He took my life and I will take his...I can't believe I said that!" I looked up, crying. "That feels good. If I could have this chance with him, I'm sure I could get on with my life."

"Do you really believe that?" Ina asked.

"If I could have gotten that knife from him that night I would have..."

"What?"

"I don't know," I admitted. "Right now, this minute, I think I could use it on him."

"Do it!"

I was sobbing. "It's too late!" I cried. "He got me first. I should be dead. I have no business here."

"Donna, you lived because you are a survivor. I admire your strength and perseverance. Just coming to see me was a move in the direction you want to go. What you have done took much courage—"

"Those words don't mean a damn thing to me!" I shouted, interrupting. "I just can't see it."

"I see it quite plainly," Ina responded. "I see a young woman, a pretty woman with a beautiful smile. She was working when a psychopath entered her store. He kidnaped her, raped her and then stabbed her. She survived the brutal attack and she sits before me believing her life is worthless."

My sobs continued. "There is some truth there, Ina. But the kidnaping was partially my fault. I've never told anyone the true story of that night." I took a ragged breath, not knowing if I could continue.

Ina reached over and patted my hand. "Tell me."

"When I was in Shock Trauma and the police were finally able to see me," I said slowly, feeling my way, "they asked what happened. I lied and told them he kidnaped me from the store. I told them he came in the store and took me out at knifepoint. I didn't want anyone to know what really happened. I didn't want my family to think I caused this thing to happen to me. What about all the people who sent me cards or the people who said prayers for me in their churches? What about those people? If anyone knew the truth, I would be looked at so much differently. I can't handle that."

"Whatever happened that night, Donna, was not your fault. This crazed maniac knew what he intended to do, and he did it. Unfortunately, it was you on the receiving end of it. If anyone is responsible for what happened that night, it is the person who attacked you. I said, *attacked you!* My goodness, you did nothing wrong."

I grimaced. "Easy for you to say. Everything I ever did as a kid was wrong. I couldn't make my bed right or wash the dishes right or mow the lawn right. I remember so many things. I can just hear them now if they knew what really happened. My father would say: 'You should have never walked out that door.' And my mother would say: 'Donna, you're alive now. You've got to get back on that horse or you will never ride again.' My mother always had a way with words," I said, rolling my eyes. "Yeah, right—get back on that horse again. I will never tell them the truth, never. I will never tell anyone. Never."

"That is very sad," Ina declared. "Why would they say those things?"

"Because my father is a damn drunk and hates any kind of intrusion in his life. What happened to me is an intrusion. You know, it gives him another reason to drink himself to a pulp. He has never been one to sit down with me and talk. Instead he points his finger and says, 'You know better.' My mother, on the other hand, has a very good heart but has never understood emotion."

"What do you mean?"

"She never allowed any of us kids to show emotion unless it was anger," I explained. "She could deal with that." I stopped short. We were really going off the subject. "I don't want to talk about my parents anymore," I said abruptly. "They are who they are and I have to live with it."

"Let's talk about that night?" Ina said, accenting the statement like a question.

I stood. "Oh, sure. You want me to tell you about that night. Whether I can trust you is the question."

"What do you mean?"

"If I tell you this thing, will you promise not to think badly of me? Will you still look at me as a courageous survivor?"

"Donna, there is nothing you can say that will change how I feel about you. I will tell you again and again—you did nothing wrong."

I was pacing. "I think I have had enough today."

"Before you leave, I need to ask you something," Ina said.

"Sure," I responded. "It's something quick, I hope, 'cause I really need to be alone."

"I need you to contract with me that you will not try to harm yourself."

I tossed my head. "I'm just angry, not suicidal. Hell, I've come this far. I wouldn't even know how to do it if I wanted to. You have my promise."

She smiled broadly. "Great! I'll see you in a couple of days. Please call me anytime if you need anything or just want to talk. I'm here for you."

"Thank you," I said, then bolted from the room...and home.

Two days later I was back in Ina's office. She welcomed me and commented on my always being on time. I was in no mood for pleasantries. "As hard as I've tried over the last couple of days," I said, "I'm still angry and upset."

"Why?" she asked. "I—"

"That's okay," I said, cutting her off. "I understand. You can't see underneath. Just this morning while I took my shower, I couldn't help looking at all my scars. They are ugly. I used to be a very muscular person. People envied my figure. I liked my figure. But now, I'm all cut up. I look like someone tried to put me back together."

"You are correct, Donna. From the outside you look very healthy."

"I'm so confused," I confessed. "I don't want to be who I am. I'm tired and sick over how I look. I'm sick of feeling scared. I just want to hide somewhere, but I don't know where. One thing is for sure, I don't want people—you know, people who know me—to feel sorry for me. This is my motivation, I think. I must maintain my outward appearance."

"Donna, I don't feel sorry for you. I think most people who know you will feel that way, too. Human nature is fragile and complex. When we see an injured animal, we want to help it. We fix it up and pray that it can make it in the wild. People want to help. With an animal we have to rely on its nonverbal communication to tell us what is wrong. With people we rely on open communication to tell us how they feel. That is exactly why we are here. Does that make any sense?"

"Yes," I replied. "We don't like to see anyone or anything suffer."

"I would like to continue where we left off last session. Would that be all right with you? Remember you were saying—"

"Oh, Jesus, Ina, do we have to?"

"I think we have to," Ina replied. "Don't you?"

"I'm starting to get angry again." *What the hell does she want from me? I hope she is not one of those people who want to hear the dirty details of what happened. No, no! I will not. I can't tell anyone.*

"Let's start with you waking up in the hospital after your attack. What was going through your mind?"

I looked at her gratefully. "That's a safe place to start. Thank you for not going to that other place. I'm not ready yet….When I woke up…hmmm…I remember, at first, I didn't know where I was. A nurse stood over my bed and I tried to talk but no words came. I felt this vacuum hose in my mouth and tried to pull it out. Of course, she stopped me. A few seconds passed before I realized where I was, but I couldn't understand why I was there. I remember asking the nurse for a piece of paper. On the paper I wrote, 'Help my friend, first, not me. She has been stabbed and raped. Where is she?'"

I shook my head, remembering. "The nurse was puzzled. She left the room and returned with a doctor who proceeded to ask me various questions. I was told to nod yes or no. He asked me if I knew where I was, asked me if I knew why I was there. He asked me what year it was. I had to put up my fingers for that. He asked me if I remembered being brought there by helicopter. I shook my head, no."

"Sounds frightening. What happened next?"

"I had this vision of a young girl lying in a pool of blood. This girl looked like me, but I couldn't really tell. I saw the whole thing happen to her, but I was paralyzed, unable to help her. She was screaming and crying out for help. I just stood there watching this whole thing happen. What a terrible sight it was. The more I moved toward helping her, the farther away I got. It was a nightmare."

"You know now the person you saw was yourself?"

"Unfortunately, yes. But at that time and at that moment, I really believed it was not me. After a few minutes of answering their questions, I realized the truth—the truth that stays deep within me."

"What is so hard for you to say out loud?" Ina asked.

Okay, here we are again, I thought. *You're trying to pull that truth out of me for your own satisfaction. Because you volunteered to tell me what happened to you, I'm supposed to tell you about me? Well, it just doesn't work that way. Not with me. I'm much smarter than that.*

Ina broke into my thoughts. "Donna, are you with me? What are you thinking about?"

"What was I just thinking about? Well, I'm getting angry at you for asking me personal questions. That's one. And two, how do I know I can trust you with such information? You could turn on me and tell my family or something."

"Everything that happens in this room stays in this room," Ina declared. "Our purpose for talking about these things is to move through it. Once you begin to tell me the truth, you will begin to work through your fear of telling it. Nothing can be as bad as what was done to you. I will reiterate: You, Donna Ferres, did nothing wrong. You were working, doing your job—which, you have explained, was very fulfilling to you—when someone came with premeditated thoughts to kidnap you, rape you and kill you. You did not ask for this thing to happen to you. You are the victim of a vicious predator. Whatever it is, we must bring it to the table."

"What you don't know is that there are several things I am ashamed of about that night. You think there is only one. Well, there are several, and I can't bring myself to tell you or anyone. Do you know these things are so strong that I can't even see what you see? I am completely going nuts over this, but I can't trust a single soul."

"Do you remember when the detectives came to the hospital?" she asked.

"Yes."

"What happened with that?"

"I think it was the first time I was allowed out of my bed. I remember getting really dizzy, and I had all these tubes hanging off me. I looked terrible. My hair was knotted and my bedclothes were wrinkled and I had a pair of slippers that kept falling off my feet. It was quite a task."

Ina smiled.

"That does sound kinda funny," I said in response to her smile. "The problem was when my slippers came off my feet, I couldn't lean over enough to put them back on. Luckily the nurse who was escorting me helped me. She was a fine nurse. I really liked her. She never put me under any pressure. She just helped me. Anyway…I was told three detectives were waiting to talk to me in a room down the hall. My first thought was, *there is no way I'm going to go into a room with three men.* I didn't care if they had badges or not. I really thought they were there to finish the job. You know. First I asked the nurse to find my sister Debbie and tell her to come in with me, but Debbie had just left. So I asked the nurse to come in with me. With her, I entered the room with the three men. They were standing around a table looking at a folder. They immediately greeted me and introduced themselves. I looked like hell. A guy named Nauman helped me over to a chair. He was a big guy, not fat, just big. Glad he was on my side. All of a sudden, sitting there, I realized I would have to tell them what happened. Good thing my sister wasn't there. She would hear the lies pouring out of me. So they asked me. I remember telling them I was on medication and I couldn't really remember too much. They seemed okay with this but insisted they would need a statement to the best of my recollection. The more they stared at me the more fright-

ened I became. I completely skipped over the kidnaping part
and went to the rape and stabbing."

Ina sat very still, watching my face and listening closely. I
continued my narrative. "Then the big question came. 'Donna,
how did he get you out of the store?' And the lies began.
Even knowing these guys were here to help me, I still lied.
There was no way I was going to tell them the truth. I told
them my attacker put the knife to my throat in the store and
carried me out. I feel so embarrassed even saying it now. I am
not a good liar. But they didn't know. They asked about the
car, about him and about the places he took me. They asked
me what sexual acts were committed and was there intercourse. Well, luckily they were filling in the blanks to many
of the questions. I just needed to say yes or no.

"Then a funny thing happened. They opened the folder.
Inside it was a statement from my attacker. I remember thinking, *Shit, I'm caught. I'm going to get into trouble*. And the big
question was asked again. 'Donna, the suspect gave us a written statement and it doesn't align with yours. Can you help
us to understand what happened at the store?' I told them I
couldn't remember too much about that part. So they read
the part of his statement that said he lured me out. And I
said yes, that's right. 'So his statement would be accurate as
to what happened?' I said yes. 'Okay, then all we need from
you now is to pick out your attacker from these six photos.' I
picked him out immediately and the detectives left. I could
tell from their expressions they knew I was hiding something,
but I had too much guilt to tell them myself."

"Donna, you did what you had to do. No one will fault
you for that. They had the attacker behind bars. He confessed, and you did what you needed to do at the time."

"I felt so alone. I was scared. I was sick. I had tubes and
scars and I just couldn't take another step back. So I lied. I
was relieved they didn't pressure me. I don't want any more
pressure. Not even here."

"Let's just say, you tell me about this thing. What do you feel would happen to you?"

"I would have a panic attack. They are not very pleasant to watch. I can't breathe. I lose complete control and my heart races viciously. I don't want to feel that right now. Just thinking about revealing that part would tear me up. No one will know, never." *This lady is just not going to quit,* I thought. *I'm going to have to make a decision—tell her or stop coming. Why am I coming anyway? I must try and figure this out. I know she means well and I think I can trust her, so what is the big deal? What is stopping me? I want to get better. I want to get back to work and forget all this. I want to tell, but I can't.*

"I can see you are feeling much pressure right now," Ina said. "Why don't we stop for the day and give you a little more time to think this over. I have you down for next Tuesday. Are you okay with that?"

"Yes. I have lots to think about," I replied. "I want to return, but I'm not sure. I can tell you this. Each time I leave, I think I feel a little bit better. I don't know what that means, but something is working. Thank you."

"It is my pleasure," Ina said. "I'm glad you told me that. I know this is very hard for you, and baby steps will get us where we need to be. Baby steps, Donna. I will see you Tuesday, then?"

"Yes."

As I drove home my mind was whirling. *What in the world am I thinking? Who is saying those words? I feel as though I have two personalities. One wants to tell Ina what she wants to hear, and the other just wants to stay mad and not trust anyone. Someone help me! I have no one to turn to, to ask what I should do. My poor family is going through their own grief, and I can't ask them what is right. My friends don't know what to say to me. Everyone is just keeping their distance, waiting for me to invite them in. Ina is all I have, and I'm not sure she is all that trustworthy. I wish I had died that night. Then I wouldn't be here with all these damn problems. Nothing I do stops me from thinking about that night. I just want it all to go away. But everything I do, everywhere I go, reminds me of it. Someone help me! Please.*

Five days passed, and once again I found myself in Ina's office. Ina ushered me in with her usual smile. "How are you doing today?" she asked. "How was your weekend?"

"Well, I wish I could tell you everything was fine. But—"

"Did something happen?"

"You could say that. A friend of mine—someone I had been going out with before my attack—called and wanted to take me out to dinner. Believe it or not, I agreed. I must have been having a good moment at the time. Well, as the day progressed and nighttime approached, things began to change my decision. Charlie came to pick me up. I was all dolled up, him too. He walked me to his van, and I got in. The minute we pulled out of the driveway I had a panic attack. He became my attacker. I yelled at him to stop the car. Of course he didn't understand what was going on. I yelled and screamed for him to let me out, let me out. The poor guy stopped the van and ran around to my side. The minute he put his hand on me I began to fight him. He backed off and let me run back to the house." I shook my head and sobbed. "What's wrong with me? Am I crazy?"

"It's just a little soon for you, that's all," Ina replied. "You are not crazy. Remember, you have lived through a violent occurrence. As with your physical injuries, your mind was traumatized. Its ability to recall is fresh and raw—"

"I just want to forget."

"That's why you are here, Donna. We must chip away at these thoughts and try to understand them. What you did the other night with Charlie is completely understandable. Did you agree to go out with him for you or for him?"

"For him, really."

"Good. This is a good beginning. By your doing this for him, it shows you felt obligated to be who you used to be. I think we both know the attack has changed you, and understandably so."

"I want my life back," I said, sobbing. "Make my mind stop, please."

"Do you remember telling me how much you enjoyed changing jobs? You had goals and plans for your future. This is where we start. You worked hard to find a new job. You work hard at everything you do, even surviving that terrible night. Now is the time we work hard together and start chipping away at these feelings."

Work hard. Yeah, I can do that, I thought. I've always been a hard worker. Everything I have I worked hard for. I can do this. I know I can. I'm not going to be an invalid all my life. I am needed to help my family. I am the one who needs to be strong and to help them when they need me. My father sure isn't the one who will be there for them. I'm ready.

Once I got my thoughts in order, I could respond to Ina. "I think you make a very important point there. You have opened up something in me, and I think I understand. I was alert through the whole attack, but I stayed strong and used my mind to guide me through. I can use my mind now to, as you say, chip away the bad stuff. Where do we start?"

"What was going through your mind when you got in the van with Charlie?"

"I was feeling good that night until the point I was alone in the van with him. All of a sudden I couldn't breathe. It was dark, and Charlie's dash lights didn't work. He wasn't talking, which made me suspicious. But looking back on it, he was never one for talking too much. As we were backing out of my driveway he sped up a little, you know, kinda in a hurry. This alarmed me. What the hell was the hurry? Suddenly I felt he had other plans for me that night. I began believing he was going to hurt me. You know, rape me. I panicked, and when he put his hand on me, I flashed back. Just like that night when my attacker pulled me from the car on the passenger side....Ina! I can't breathe!"

Quickly handing me a paper bag, Ina commanded, "Blow into the bag slowly. Exhale."

Breathe, Donna, breathe, I told myself. *Think only about the bag and breathing. Slow breaths. Clear your mind. Don't let this happen. Slow breaths. Slow breaths.*

"Keep breathing," Ina said. After a few minutes she asked, "How we doing?"

"A little better," I replied. "I feel as though I've been run over by a Mack truck. My whole body aches. I'm going to keep this bag. It helped me to catch my breath. I never knew I could use a bag. Thank you very much. I'm feeling a little more relaxed now."

"You are very welcome. I want to give you a few more minutes and then we will talk again."

"Thank you," I said softly. "You are very kind." Sobbing, I said, "You are all I've got."

Several minutes later Ina asked, "How are you doing now?"

"Better. I'm ready to continue. Poor Charlie. I feel so bad he had to see that. I feel bad for everyone who has seen me act that way. Everyone must think I am completely nuts. I just can't help it."

"Donna, it is nothing to be ashamed of. I'm sure everyone understands. They just don't know what to say to help you."

"You have hit it right on the head. You are so smart. They just don't know what to say. Thank you for that. I learn something new every time we meet."

"Donna, what you just said is a very good example of what we are doing here. Slowly, you are beginning to consume new information—information that is positive. In our sessions you will begin to chip away at the vivid memories of your attack with positive thoughts of understanding. You are the only one who knows how you felt that night. We need to dissect these feelings and talk about them."

"Okay," I agreed in a small voice

"Are you feeling up to it?"

"I'm ready. I mean I'm really ready....You know, the store."

"Okay. Let's start there," Ina agreed.

"I just wanted to get my work done that night. It was three-thirty in the morning, a slow time for customers. This was the time I made my store look pretty—straighten and dust the shelves, bring all the merchandise forward, make everything look real full. After that I would sweep and mop, giving my floor the best shine ever, because at five o'clock all hell broke loose. Construction workers with their dirty shoes, businessmen and just early birds would begin to flock in....But that night I wouldn't see my regular customers....He came in."

I took a deep breath. "I was always pleasant to all my customers, even if they were a little weird. I would smile and give each person the best customer service. This guy brought his purchase up to the counter and told me he knew my sister. Damn!"

"What are you feeling?" Ina asked quickly.

"Having this information made me trust this guy a little," I replied. "Not that I didn't trust him. He just looked weird. He talked for a few minutes about my sis and asked how she was doing. I told him fine. You know, small talk. Then he left. I was happy, I had work to do. I can't be socializing on company time. I was glad he left. So I went into the back room and filled my bucket to mop the floor. When I came back out I noticed his car was still in the parking lot. I don't know why

I did this, but I made a safe drop—you know, dropped money into the safe. This is how I was trained. I kept my eyes on his car. I could only see a shadow. I didn't know if he was looking at me or what. I didn't feel too nervous at the time, so I proceeded to do my cleaning. Then the buzzer on the door went off and there he was again....Ina, I need a minute. Maybe the bag. I'll just hold it. I can feel my heart racing a bit."

"Take your time, Donna. Are you in the store now with him?"

"Yes. He was standing very close to me....I retreated behind the counter for protection. For a second I remembered telling one of my police friends if they ever came to the store and I wasn't there, they would find me in the ice dispenser. I was just joking around at the time, but for some odd reason I thought about that. I was playing it cool. Very professional. Then he asked if I would help him start his car. I told him I would call someone for him but I wouldn't be able to help him. So he proceeded to tell me the problem. He told me he didn't have any money to call anyone. He said it would just take a minute for him to set the points, and all I needed to do was jolt the ignition. I remember thinking about what to do as I thought about the many things still left undone in the store. I sure didn't have the money to lend him to call a tow truck. When I gazed back out the window I noticed he had a Chevy Nova, just like my car. I thought about my friend Michael who taught me all about cars. I knew what a simple and quick job this would be. So...Ina, I went out to his car. The biggest mistake I have ever made. Can't you see?" I asked, sobbing. "It was all my fault."

"Easy on yourself. Would you believe me if I told you he would have grabbed you anyway? He had already figured in his mind what he was going to do, with or without your co-operation. If you hadn't followed him out to his car, he would have grabbed you from inside the store. You must believe that.

"He tricked me. That son-of-a-bitch tricked me. Oh, how I struggled to get back into my store after I figured out what was going on. Once he pulled that knife out and cut my pinky finger almost off, I knew I was in real trouble. Why would he want to hurt someone like me?"

"It wasn't personal. He knew what he was going to do that night whether it was you or someone else. I really believe if it had been someone else, she probably would not have survived."

"Then she would be lucky. Who in her right mind would want to live after such a terrible experience? I live with this thing over and over again. Everywhere I go, every smell, every person I see and every noise I hear. It is constantly in my head. I can't concentrate. I can't feel enjoyment just waiting for another attack to occur. I'm vulnerable to life's every move."

"Donna, do you realize you just told me what happened at the store?"

"Yes, but while I told you, I didn't even see you in the room. I was watching from above, in the store. I saw him come in and heard him talk. I went outside and I could feel the blood running down my finger. You weren't even here."

"Well, I was here," Ina replied, "and I heard you loud and clear. Now let me tell you what I heard. I heard a dedicated employee just wanting to get her routine assignments completed. I heard you speak of wanting to help a person who acknowledged being a friend of her sister. I heard you speak of having knowledge about cars, especially about Chevy Novas. I heard you speak from your heart, a heart that has always been there to help others, a good heart. I heard your fear when you figured out what was going on. Donna, you did not ask this man to do these things to you. You did not cause these things to happen to you."

"I wish I could believe that."

"We'll keep at it," Ina promised. "In time, you will see. Remember this is just the beginning."

"Thank you. I think I have had enough today," I said. "I just want to go home and rest."

"Okay. You have had a rough day. I'll see you on Thursday."

"Yes, Thursday."

In two days I was back again.

Ina began with a question. "How have you been feeling since our last session?"

"I'm doing okay, I guess," I replied. "Telling you about the store, well, I thought I would feel better, but I feel more vulnerable. You know…Jesus! I'm always watching my back. For example, yesterday I went to the grocery store, just a couple of blocks from my house, and I was so paranoid with the people around me I couldn't concentrate on what I was doing there, so I left. My hands were trembling so bad I couldn't get the key into my car door, thinking any minute someone was going to come up behind me."

"What are you feeling right now?"

"Angry, that once I get comfortable here I have to leave. I hate leaving this building. I have to walk down the long hallway, then out to the parking lot. Heaven forbid I need to get into an elevator. No way that could happen! Just thinking about it makes me feel like I can't breathe. I'm just scared all the time. What happened to me that night can never happen to me again. I mean never, 'cause if it does, they'd better kill me. I am so mad I didn't die that night. This is bullshit. What kind of life do I have? I can't see beyond the next minute. I want so much to be able to do something…even read! But my concentration is short and I get frustrated. I don't feel safe anywhere. Even here I can hear the door open in the waiting room and then for several minutes I wait for some-one to come barging in with a gun to kill me. You could be in danger just being around me."

Ina cleared her throat. "Donna...I have a friend who is a psychiatrist. I've talked to her about your case, and we both feel it would be important for you to see her. We feel that maybe medication will help reduce some of your anxiety. What do you think about that?"

"Can't you just do it yourself?"

"I'm not a medical doctor, so I can't prescribe medica-tion."

"Then I don't need it. I really don't want to go through my story all over again with someone new. It's hard enough just telling you. Isn't there another way?"

"I've explained to her about your attack, and she under-stands what you have been through," Ina said. "She will basically ask you questions. You can answer what you feel comfortable with."

"Do you think doing this will help me get better faster?"

"I think it is where we need to go. I will continue seeing you for therapy, and she will manage your medications. So would you like me to give her a call and set it up?"

Things are moving way too fast for me. Who is this psychia-trist? I wondered. *I have enough damn doctors right now. What should I do? Whatever I do, it has to be for me. What should I do? Oh, how I wish I had someone to ask. Why can't I answer for myself? Someone help me!*

"Donna, are you okay?"

"I can't answer that!" I snapped. "It is too hard a question. I just want to go home."

"I'm sorry if I upset you. What is bothering you right now?"

"You're trying to get rid of me. You want to push me off to someone else, don't you? This is just great. Now I've told you what I did, you are starting to feel exactly what I said you were going to feel. You're getting sick and tired of hearing my self-loathing, aren't you?"

"Oh, Donna, where is this coming from? I am not going to abandon you. I am here for as long as you need me. I have become very close to you and want to help you get through this. I'm not going anywhere. As a matter of fact, I was wondering if you would like to stay after your session and answer phones for me. There is always room for another hand around here, and I think you would be perfect. What do you think?"

"Really? Did you just think that up?" I asked suspiciously.

"Nope," she assured me. "I've been thinking about it. We get lots of calls and I could use you."

"What if I'm out there alone and someone comes in? I'd flip out. Wouldn't be good for business. Thanks, but I don't think I'm up to it. Just the thought of someone coming in would freak me out. I'll tell you this, if ever in my future I get better, I will take you up on that offer. I wish I had had a woman to talk to when I was being interviewed, instead of those three men. When I lay on those strangers' porch with only my panties on, with policemen and firemen all around me—I know I was bloodied and beaten, but I still remember—not one woman was there. Before I was covered, the paramedics started an IV and took blood pressures while I lay there...nearly naked."

"Tell me more?" Her statement was a question.

"Dammit!" I swore, crying. "Those people made me sit on their porch. I was dying, and they made me walk up their damn stairs to their porch on the side of the house. How inhumane! And when I asked for a drink of water, they put in on the porch and wouldn't come near me. I had to get up and get it myself. Of course, I looked a hideous mess. They were an older couple. They just stared at me through their glass doors. I asked them to call my mother, and I think I gave them her number. I needed to be comforted. You know, like right before you die. It never works out like that, but just sitting here thinking about it makes me wish someone had comforted me. I was dying, and these people just watched."

"Sometimes people just don't know what the right thing is to do," Ina said. "I'm sorry that happened."

"I don't know why I thought of that," I said. "These thoughts just pop into my head. Most times I'm alone and have no one to talk to about them. See, we were talking about something completely different when this popped into my head. I can't get away from it."

"Sometimes medication can help. It will help to reduce your anxiety by slowing down your thought processes. Why don't we give it a try?"

"Are you sure this lady is okay?"

"I've known her for a long time and have been referring my clients to her with no complaints. I'm sure you'll do fine. I can call her and get everything set up if you like."

"Where is she located?"

"I could have her see you at the hospital. That way I would be close by if you needed me. Will that be okay?"

"I'll try it."

"I will try to schedule the appointment with her right before mine next week," Ina said. "That way you won't need to make the extra drive, plus you can tell me how it went."

"I guess that's okay with me."

My mind was churning. *I feel like a three-year-old. One minute I want to be an adult, the next minute I can't do a thing for myself. I trust Ina. I know she wouldn't steer me wrong. She must think this lady is okay, or she would never have brought it up. I can't go back on my word now. Stop it, Donna. You are doing this for you, no one else. You want to get better. Just do it.*

"You've gotten quiet," Ina said. "Are you doing all right?"

"I'm just tired, that's all. I think I want to go home now," I replied.

"All right. I'll call you tomorrow and tell you where you need to be on Tuesday. Her name is Emily Krauss. I think you will like her."

"Emily, that's a nice name," I commented.

"Yes, it is," Ina agreed. "So I will see you next week and I'll call you tomorrow....I'll walk you out. I've got to drop some files off at the administration office across the street."

"That would be great."

Ina is so cool, I thought. *I know she doesn't have any files. She just wants to walk me out. See what happens when you tell people stuff. This is a nice thing; accept it. People want to do nice things for you.*

At the next session with Ina, five days later, she greeted me with the question, "How did it go?"

Coming straight from my visit with Emily Krauss, I had a positive attitude. "Very well, thank you," I said, smiling at Ina. "Thanks for setting this up at the hospital. It saved me from going to a new area. I liked her. A little older than what I expected, but good. She didn't ask me anything personal about my attack. She only wanted to know about my sleep, panic attacks, eating habits—those sorts of things, so I told her about my night sweats, nightmares, lack of appetite and stuff like that."

"You never told me about these things."

"No, um—"

"Do you have your medication?"

"Yes. It's called Pamelor. I'll try it."

"Good."

"Good."

"When will you see her again?" Ina asked.

"Three weeks. We talked about setting it up the same way, at the hospital."

"Good. You ready to get to work now?"

"Ready." I nodded as I answered.

"We left last session with you telling about sitting on the porch of the house you went to. How did you get to that house? Why that house?"

"I can sum that up in one word. Dog! Did you know that dog spelled backward is god? After my attacker left me lying in a pool of blood, wait...I need some Kleenex." Tears welled in my eyes. "I just can't stand seeing myself like that. Um...that bastard! He tried to kill me...." I began to cry. "I'm a nice person," I said through my sobs. I could hear my voice getting high and tight as I went on. "Why would he do this to me? I told him I wouldn't tell."

Ina's voice softly came to me. "Cry it out. Let it go. Let it go."

He stabbed me. Why didn't it hurt? Right through my skin. The squishing sound into my back. The blood running down my side. The dog barking. He helped me. My good friend. My good friend.

"I'll be all right," I said, blowing my nose. "You see, Ina, the dog led me out. I followed his barking and that led me out."

"Was the dog at this house?"

"No, I never saw the dog. Once I got out to the street, the barking stopped. I never saw the dog to thank him for saving my life. You see, when I was lying in the woods, I was nearly blind—not just from not having my glasses. He had also thrown sand all over my face and in my eyes. I had no idea where I was. The darkness and thickness of the woods prevented me from knowing there were houses nearby. I heard the dog and followed the sound....No one will ever know what it took for me to get through those woods. Every tree branch that I stood on cracked so loud I thought for sure my attacker would figure out I was not dead and would come back. The more I worried about that, the more aggressive I became getting through the woods."

I paused, wiping the bottom edges of my eyes. "There was no path," I continued. "I had to make my own. I mean, tearing through sticker bushes so thick I had to use my whole body like a bulldozer—my face, legs, arms and chest to push my way through. At one point there was a dead tree in my path. I couldn't go forward or backward, so I had no choice but to lift the trunk up off the ground and go underneath it. It was the barking that gave me the strength to continue. When I dropped the tree, the sound was so loud I thought for sure he was standing right behind me, and I screamed. I could feel the blood flowing out of my wounds with every step I took. My body was torn up. Stickers stuck in my skin and hair. Dammit, I was scared out of my mind, but I kept going."

Ina interrupted. "Let's take a few seconds."

This time, I was the one who didn't want to stop. My words tumbled out. "It was so scary. Frightening, you know? I knew if he caught me it was over for me and—" I screamed, so enmeshed was I in the scene I was reliving.

"Get it out," Ina encouraged me.

"Oh, my God. I gotta go home. I'm scared. I've got to get to a safe place."

"You are safe here, Donna. Let's talk about now. You are in my office. You have been seeing me for some time now and nothing bad has happened to you. I'm right here. No one is going to hurt you. Look around the room. You know this cluttered room. You are sitting in the same chair you always sit in when you come."

"I understand." I was breathing heavily. "I can't breathe....The bag! The bag!"

Ina handed me the bag. "Slowly...deep breaths. Slowly, now. Close your eyes, relax, breathe slowly and think of a safe place. A place where there is no evil. A peaceful place without violence. Relax. Are you thinking?"

I was concentrating on breathing slowly as I answered, "Uh huh."

"Would you like to share with me the place that helped you?"

"It was heaven. At least, the heaven I've always imagined," I replied. "Children and dogs everywhere. The sky is blue and I feel completely safe. The air is clean. No noise, no loud annoyances and no people. Just calm. Just calm." My eyes were closed. "Just calm."

"Sounds like a very nice place. Are you still there?"

"Yes. And this is where I want to stay. No more talking of that terrible world below me. I want to be free. Free to be who I used to be. I want to be free."

"You are."

I began to cry again. "No, I'm not. I'm in the woods. Every step is so loud. The damn dead branches and leaves keep cracking louder and louder."

"The dog, Donna. Can you hear the dog?"

"Yes, he is there guiding me out. Oh, my little friend. My little friend. Thank you so much for helping me." *Concentrate on the dog*, I told myself as the memories held me in their grip. *Stop thinking about the woods. The dog is here to help you. The dog. The wonderful dog. I love that dog. Thank you. Thank you. I never said thank you.*

"Donna?"

"I'm okay. I'm okay. I'm here in your office." I opened my eyes. "You are my friend. You are there for me. Thank you. I don't know if I can go to the woods anymore. It's a frightening place, and I don't like it."

"Yes, it is a frightening place," Ina said.

"I want so bad to be angry, but instead I feel so damn sorry for myself. I almost can't bear it. I'm sure there are so many other people who have been through much more than I have. What right do I have to feel this way?"

"You have been through a terrible ordeal, Donna. Unfortunately, this is something you cannot just snap out of. It takes time and hard work—tears, screams, getting angry. It's a process. You can't just get over it. You have to get through it. It's the same process for others who have been through similar or other tragedies."

"Yes, I guess you are right."

"Would you like to stop now?" Ina asked.

"Yes. Thank you for today."

"You're welcome. I will see you on Thursday, then?"

Two days later I was back in Ina's office, hearing her usual opening question: "How are you doing today?"

"I started taking my medicine and it's been making me nauseous. Debbie got real concerned and wanted to take me to the hospital. She thought it had something to do with my intestines. She takes such good care of me. But I told her I thought it was probably from the medicine. I slept pretty well, though. I didn't wake up at all."

"You're going to see Dr. Krauss three weeks from Tuesday, right?"

"Right. Yesterday while I was home, someone knocked on my door. As usual, I peeked around the corner and looked through the curtains to see who it was. It was a lady, a middle-aged lady. I had never seen her before, but I asked her through the door what she wanted. She told me she lived across the street and was wondering if she could talk to me. I couldn't decide what to do— if I should open the door or just tell her to go away. The old Donna would have eagerly opened the door. So I waited several minutes trying to figure out what to do. I needed more information on what this was all about.

"She then backed away from the door about 10 feet. When she did this I opened the door, quickly looking to both sides to make sure this wasn't some kind of setup to lure me out. I only opened the door enough to be able to see her while she talked. She said she had heard what had happened to me and for several weeks she had tried to get the courage to come over and tell me how sorry she was to hear about it. I thanked her, but she wanted more. She wanted me to come over to her house and talk with her. She said she had two daughters in their teens and she wanted to know from me what she could tell them so something like this would never happen to them."

"What did you do?" Ina asked.

"I took a chance, that's what I did. I hadn't been out of the house except to come see you or go to the doctor...and that one time to the grocery store. I couldn't decide in my mind what to do, so I followed my heart. If I could help this lady, I wanted to. So I went over to her house. Scared ...guarded. She was a very nice lady. She seemed very concerned for her daughters. I didn't go too far into her house. I stood, like, in the house but right at the front door so I could make my escape if I needed to."

"What did you tell her?"

"I told her not to alarm her daughters by making them afraid of every person who is nice to them. I told her that instead, she should communicate with her daughters about how they react to certain situations. I told her to tell her daughters they must follow their instincts. If a situation is the least bit uncomfortable, not to do it. If there is that slight doubt, say no, even if the person is persistent. This is where you, the mom, come in—communication. Ask them if they have ever been in a situation like that and ask them what they did. Did they give in or did they stick to their guns? Their answers will help you to understand who they are and

how they react in social settings. So with that, I started to
leave. She thanked me and wanted to hug me, so I put out
my hand and we shook hands. I was feeling pretty good about
what I said and proud I didn't screw it up. I was proud of
myself that I was able to keep a single thought and follow it
through. So many times I could be talking and completely
forget what I'm talking about. But I did it."

"Donna, it sounds like real good advice."

"I wish someone had given me that kind of advice. You
know, like my parents communicating with me about the
real world. Shit, I was only 24. I didn't know about getting
raped. That was probably the last thing that ever crossed my
mind that night. My friends never talked about it. It just never
happened in my circle of friends or family. So when it happened to me…well, you know what happened. Anyway, when
I left her house and was heading home, I noticed my sister's
car in the driveway. I knew she was going to be worried, so I
tried my hardest to hurry home. I still can't move very fast
because of my scar. When I got to the top of the driveway
she came running out of the house and hugged me. She told
me she called the cops because my car was there and I wasn't.
She thought someone came and got me again. I felt so bad
for her. I should have realized she would come home from
work as she always does to check up on me. Then I did something stupid like that. No note or anything. She was in sheer
panic. So we ran back in the house and called the police back
and told them it was a false alarm and apologized."

"So you have been busy," Ina commented.

"Deb had a real adrenalin rush, if you know what I mean.
Then she had to go back to work. Something like that really
makes you tired. I felt so bad. I should have known better.
The last person in the world I would ever want to upset is
her. She has helped me so much. I feel so bad about that."

"I'm sure your sister was so pleased to see you she forgot all about the panic she was feeling," Ina assured me. "You are very lucky to have her."

"Yes, you are so right. Good things do happen."

"Yes, they do," I agreed.

Time passed, and the year turned to 1980; still I continued my sessions with Ina. She was my lifeline, increasingly so, since those who were once close to me could not seem to understand why I could not move on. Well, if they had asked—and if I could have answered—I'd have told them I didn't understand it, either. Why couldn't I just get over it? I felt that Debbie and Barbara were becoming as impatient as my mother, although they carefully hid their feelings.

One morning in February after Ina's usual opening question, I answered, "I'm feeling good. I'm ready to go to work."

"Where would you like to go today?" Ina asked.

"I just told you. I want to go back to work. I'm getter braver…taking chances. Maybe I should think about working again."

"What do you have in mind?"

"I think I want to finish my rotation at the store and move up the fast-track ladder. I know I'm saying that, but I don't even know if they would take me back. I want to get back into it. Am I totally nuts or what?"

"Why go back there?"

"That's all I know. I remember the paperwork, the work itself, the customers, you know? I liked it. I can't just sit around for the rest of my life and mope. I'll ask for days and make sure I will always have someone with me. No one would dare hurt me with other people around….would they?"

"I'm just afraid it might be too soon."

"It's been six months!" I protested. "My injuries are better. I'm on medication for panic attacks. I think right this moment I can do it."

"What would you have to do to get back on the job?" Ina asked.

"I guess I could call my district manager and talk to him."

Ina's hesitation was clear as she spoke. "Well, if you feel that strongly—"

"Okay!" I exclaimed, interrupting her. "I'm going to do that right now while I'm feeling good." I stood. "So I will see you next Tuesday. I'll let you know what happens."

"All right," Ina said. "Promise me you won't make any commitments 'til you see me again. I think we should talk about it more—"

"Okay! I'm going to do this thing."

As I rushed out, I thought about what I was about to do. *I'm going to make the call....Are you insane? I'll say, "Hello, this is Donna Ferres." No. "Hi, this is Donna Ferres. I was wondering if I still have a job?" Okay, that's a good way to put it. Don't be nervous. They are probably going to flip when they find out who it is. Who in their right mind would want to return to the same store they were almost murdered in? Got to get back on that horse. I've got to do this. I need the money. I need to be productive...I must be out of my mind. No one has offered me a job or has helped me with finances, so what am I supposed to do? Let's think about this. If I don't do this thing then I have to worry about getting another kind of job. But what kind of other job? If I have to interview, what do I tell them I've been doing over the last six months? Oh, yeah, that would go over real big. They would hire me in a minute. This way if I go back to my old job I won't have to worry about all that other stuff. I could just walk in and do my job. I wouldn't have to explain anything to anybody about anything. This is good. Okay! I've made up my mind...I think. I'll just see how it goes.*

"Good morning, Donna. How are you doing?" Ina asked as I came into the room for our session five days later.

"Lousy. I'm so damn depressed. I could hardly make it here today."

"Has something happened over the weekend?"

"I don't know if you remember when I left here Thursday. I was feeling really good. You know, gung ho about going back to work and forgetting all this bullshit."

"Yes, I remember. Did you make the call?"

"Well…" Tears came to my eyes. "I drove to the store, the convenience store. I pulled into a back parking space so no one would see me, and do you know what I saw?"

"No, tell me."

"I saw everyone was going on with their lives. Can you imagine that? Customers rushing inside to get their morning coffee and paper. Mothers getting school supplies, milk and bread. Business as usual."

"Why did that upset you?"

"Because I used to be a part of it. Working quickly to move these customers out the door so as not to make them wait. I used to be really good at it—making coffee, waiting on customers, making small talk and meeting their morning needs. I could only watch, but the momentum of my past was real. I really enjoyed my work. Now I can only watch from a distance."

"How long did you stay?"

"Not too long. I could see eyes looking in my direction. You know, people associate you with the car you drive…and I think they were suspicious it was me. So I left."

"Then what did you do, Donna?"

"I wanted to die. I was so sad, I thought I *would* die. Instead I went the route."

"The route," Ina repeated, puzzled. "What route is that?"

"I went to the scene of the crime. Scared out of my mind. I couldn't find the backyard where he raped me, but I did find the dirt road in the gravel area and drove back there. I sat in my car for a very long time, then opened my door and walked down a ways. Then all hell broke loose." I started sobbing.

"Was this the first time you've been there since the attack?"

"Yes. I was wondering how I could go back to the store without knowing what this place looked like in the daytime. That's why I went, but it was a real mistake. I lay on the ground curled in a fetal position, and I cried out, 'Let me die! Let me die!'"

Ina offered me a Kleenex and waited a moment before speaking. "When did you do this?"

"Friday, the day after I saw you. If I had never walked out of the store, I wouldn't be in this mess. I brought this on myself! I'm ruined. I can't do a damn thing. I come here and spill my guts about guilt and shame and still I can't do a damn thing. I'll never amount to anything. I should have died that night. Why didn't I die?"

"I think what you did was very brave," Ina said. "Returning to that area must have been very scary for you. Especially going alone. Can you tell me what was going through your mind as you lay there?"

"I just wanted to be dead. I couldn't think of one person I'd have wanted to share this with, and that is a real shame. No one understands anything. How can I go on, having no one in my life except my family? And I refuse to burden them with this. The more I want to, the more I reject them. They will never understand. They can't help me. No one can help me but myself, and I'm just too weak to go on. I should be dead, damn it, dead! I will never get over this thing. I just want it all to go away or I want to die. These are the only two choices I have."

"What can I do?" Ina asked.

"I need a bodyguard," I replied. "I obviously can't protect myself. I would like to have someone who will stay with me all the time and protect me. Except I don't know who I can trust or who has the time. Maybe that damn psychiatrist from Shock Trauma was right. I need to be in a mental hospital. I could just stay there and behave crazy all the time. I'd be fed, watered and not bothered with. That sounds like a good idea."

"Do you really think so, Donna?"

"No. No…but I don't know what I need."

"Let's start with talking about getting you into something," Ina suggested. "Do you have any hobbies? Things you like to do?"

"I like to work. I want to work."

"Okay, let's start there. What would you like to do?"

"I want to make money again. I'm poor. I want a degree in something. Problem is, I can't even imagine interviewing. How could I explain my time off from work? I wouldn't dare tell any new employer what happened. Just the thought of interviewing makes me nervous because I'm not a very good liar."

"Okay, that's a good start. Do you think your company would take you back in a new position? Maybe receptionist or something like that?"

"I don't know. Receptionist doesn't sound like me. But I guess I could give it a try."

"Good. Why don't you give your district manager a call today and make an appointment. This way you can put your thoughts on paper and take it with you. He already knows what you have been through, so you wouldn't need to go into that. Maybe he may even have some ideas for you."

"I guess that sounds reasonable," I said slowly. "I think I could do that if I could put up with the stares from the district office employees. They all know me, you know. I used to have to drop paperwork off all the time, and they all know me....I'll hold my head up high and keep my mind on the subject. I think I could do that. Anyway, they are all nice people. I get along with everyone there."

"It sounds like a plan," Ina declared. "So you will call today when you get home. Make the appointment, and we will take it from there. You can call me with the information, and I will make it a point to be available when you get done. You're smiling. That's a good sign."

"I just had a moment of pleasure. And you know, it really felt good. I feel as though we have accomplished something instead of dragging all that other stuff into it. I don't like to talk about that other stuff. It wears me out and makes me upset, but setting goals is good. I like the way it feels, and most of all, you and I worked on it together. You, I can trust. You, I can trust because you don't feel sorry for me. You have helped me to have a reason for living."

"If this session helped you through all that, then we together can get you what you want. We will work as long and as hard as it takes. Today, you smiled."

"I'd like to go now," I said. "I want to reflect on this feeling while it's still fresh in my mind. Thank you so much for everything. I feel much better knowing I have options. I won't have to sit around the house all day and think. I need to work. I have bills to pay, and I want to help my sister."

"That sounds fine with me. I'll be available, Donna, so please call. You did real well today. So, I will see you on Thursday?"

I nodded.

"Good luck, Donna."

Returning to Work

I never saw Ina again. The medication was working, and once I began working days, I was unable to see her during the day. Emotionally, I was simply not able to go out after dark, although I'm sure she would have made evening appointments for me. Choosing to stop seeing Ina was a decision I would regret in times to come. My goals had changed and "not doing too much too soon" was the good advice with which Ina left me. Entering the real world for me was learning to trust again, learning to communicate again and most of all, learning to live in a world full of people.

I fulfilled my promise to myself by talking to my district manager, Bill Meyer. As I expected, the employees were amazed and shocked to see me appear again. They were, of course, all cordial, but they had that look about them. And I can understand that. In a separate room, Bill and I discussed my returning to work. I wasn't nervous being alone with him. He was a little guy, harmless, very gracious…but nervous. I couldn't blame the man. Here I was asking to come back to a place that could send me into a frenzy of post-traumatic stress. You didn't need to be a rocket scientist to figure that out. Yet he was willing to give me anything I wanted.

I weighed the employment options he provided to me, which were many, from receptionist to posting clerk or financing, or returning to the convenience store. We talked for a long time, and I explained my goal still was to work toward management. I said this, knowing it would put me right back into the store, the place that changed my life. He detailed my new responsibilities, and we were able to compromise without changing corporate protocol. I didn't want any freebies or special attention. We both agreed I would work daytime hours, always with another employee. We shook hands. It was final. I would begin work the following Monday.

The decision was mine alone, and I had to take responsibility for it. I knew I owed it to my family to explain to them why. I asked my mom and sisters to meet with me as I prepared myself for some major opposition. I decided to meet with my father separately.

We sat around my mother's kitchen table. They had no idea what was on my mind, but I knew I needed to be as positive as possible so I wouldn't upset anyone. They had been through enough, and I wanted to leave them believing I was strong enough to do this. I just blurted it out. Everyone sat there with their mouths open, not knowing how to respond.

"Oh, Donna," my mother cried. "Are you sure you want to do that? Can't you work somewhere else?"

I put my arm around her and tried to explain. "This is the only thing I know, Mom, and I must return to it. Getting another job is no option. Interviewing with other companies would only open old wounds, and I'm not strong enough to explain why I quit my old job. Too much explanation would be necessary—explanation I'm not willing or ready to reveal." My mother became quiet, but she looked toward my sisters for their support.

Debbie, of course, had seen the worst, and she was the most concerned. "I don't want another phone call or police coming to the house telling me you're dead!" she screamed.

"It won't happen again," I assured her. I explained the conversation I had with the district manager and what my new duties would entail.

"I don't know, Donna," Debbie said more calmly.

"Look, I'm flat broke," I declared. "I need to make a move and get back to work. My health is better, and I'm ready to work."

Barbara's reaction was much more affectionate. "I can understand that," she said. "If you feel that strongly about it, then I'll back you a hundred percent."

"Thanks, Barbara. I appreciate your having confidence in my decision," I responded.

The others finally came around and gave me their support as well. We hugged, and we didn't talk about it again.

I saw my father the following morning in his haven, the basement of his home. I had never warmed to the woman he married after his divorce from Mom, and I didn't bother going through "her part" of the house. Instead I went straight to the basement, which my dad had remodeled with a built-in bar, large 25-inch TV set and a recliner. He was sitting at the bar when I arrived. He offered me a drink, which I refused, but he had one. It was never just beer with him anymore. I couldn't imagine what it felt like to have a drink at 10 in the morning.

I told him I had something serious to talk to him about and I needed his full attention. His wife stayed upstairs. I was glad, because this was between me and my dad.

"What's up, kid?" This is the way he always addressed me. He had that look in his eyes that made me nervous. One could never predict how quickly he might get angry over something. He probably thought I was going to ask for something. Hell, I knew better than that. He was the same father that, when my car was broken down on the side of the road with a flat tire, came to help but made it clear I was on my own in the future. I was to learn how to change a tire and not call him again.

Now I looked at him with no love in my heart. I couldn't believe I was wasting my time talking to him. He had never really been a father to me. Everything was booze, booze, booze. Maybe once in a while he would act as though he cared, but it came infrequently. I started to get mad but remembered I felt obligated to tell him. I told him I had decided to return to work and I wanted his blessing.

"Let's celebrate!" he proposed.

I wasn't shocked at his comment. His blasé attitude pissed me off, so I told him to have another drink on me and began to leave.

"Wait, Donna, what's your hurry?" he asked.

I didn't answer. I knew this was a subject he didn't want to deal with. He had never sat down with me on any issue as a kid or adult.

"What are you going to be doing?" he pressed. "Did you go back to the factory?" He was smiling, and I knew he was, as always, looking for me to fail. I felt certain he'd have been very happy to see me go back to the factory. I felt nothing for him. All that I have been through, and this was the attitude I was getting. He really had no concept of what I was telling him.

I am your daughter, for God's sake! He doesn't even realize I drove here all alone, and he doesn't care....Donna, you are beginning to get angry and your breathing is getting short. Control yourself. Too many other important things need to be done. Don't worry about him. He will never change, and he will never give you the love you need from him. You know this. Don't expect it. Just finish what you're doing here and leave.

"Well, Dad, I just stopped by to tell you I'm going back to the convenience store and I start on Monday. I just wanted you to know. I don't need your approval, although it would be nice. I have made my decision, and that's what I came by to tell you."

"You can't be serious."

"Oh, I'm very serious," I assured him. "Dad, I don't have two pennies to rub together. Poor Debbie has to take care of everything. I can't keep taking from her. I have to do this, and I *must* do this. Little do you know what is going on with me. You've never asked. But that's okay. You've never wanted to know. I came to you today out of respect, because you are my father. I'm going to go now. Goodbye."

He made no comment as I left, but I felt good about what I had said. I tried not to dwell on my conversation with my father, even though it made me angry he was drinking. I had known it wasn't going to be easy, and it wasn't. My father never offered me anything. No advice, suggestions, money...most of all, he offered no support. I knew I was on my own; that was how it had always been. Was I surprised? No. Everything I've gotten in my life, I have gotten myself. I learned to be a self-starter back when I was a wet-nosed kid. I knew I could do this on my own, and I did.

I returned to work. The manager, Diana, a young, gentle-hearted person, greeted me as I arrived. The minute I came through the doors, the memories of that night clouded my thoughts, but I never let on to anyone how I was feeling. They were expecting to pay me for a job, and I was going to give it to them, no matter what. In the course of the day my mind was invaded by flashbacks, panic attacks and crying spells. I would gingerly retreat to the back room and breathe into a paper bag and get my thoughts together. It was more difficult than I could have imagined, but I hung tight. I put on a good act, but inside I was dying. I had made this decision, and I had to live with it. On the outside I was cordial, smiling and polite. I worked the aesthetics of the store to keep me away from working behind the counter while Diana, as sweet as she was, handled the customers. The first day was hell. I don't know what I expected; I felt embarrassed for myself. I knew this was a stupid idea, yet keeping busy took my mind off these feelings.

The panic attacks increased the more time I spent in the store. When I would see a Nova pull into the parking lot or someone would come up behind me while I was dusting shelves, my body would go into a startle response, prompting visions of the attack in my head. Some customers remembered me but didn't have much to say. I knew what everyone was thinking. I could read their eyes. They were wondering, as everyone else was, why in the hell I came back. It bothered me, but I had too much other stuff to deal with.

My first paycheck was sweet. I filled the refrigerator with food and bought my sister some flowers. That made things a little easier for me. I used up the entire check on paying bills and buying food, with nothing left for myself. It felt good to finally be able to chip away at my bills. In addition, I was able to run a grocery bill up to $50.00 at the store, so I could eat and drink and pay it off monthly.

Once the police officers and paramedics knew I had returned, they flocked to the store in my honor. One officer who was engaged to be married was putting the moves on me. He was so good-looking, but I knew it was only an infatuation that would pass. Some men, I felt, wanted to protect me, which was fine with me. The more they hung around the store and flirted with me the more secure I felt. Their presence helped me to overcome my fear of working behind the counter. Calvin, the paramedic who saved my life, visited me quite often. He was the quick-thinking man who had made the decision to send me by helicopter to Shock Trauma. I had a certain bond with him—one only he and I shared. He would sit on a grocery tote, read the paper and stay with me while

Diana ran to the bank. I knew in my heart what he was doing, and I was grateful. He was someone I could trust.

One day while I was making coffee, three police officers came in. I smiled at them as I did all my other customers. I had seen one of them before, but only enough to say hello. They obviously knew who I was. As I was leaning over to remove an empty pot from the machine, one officer, a big-bellied, slob-like person, made a comment. I could hear him clearly when he said, "He didn't like her wearing glasses." He was laughing as he said it. I couldn't believe my ears. *Was he talking about my attacker breaking my glasses in half? How would he know about my glasses? Did he come in the store to harass me?* The laughing echoed in my head louder and louder. I turned and looked at him with fire in my eyes. *How unprofessional can you get?* I wanted to ask the question out loud, but instead I was silent, continuing my coffee-making. It didn't stop there.

This time he addressed the question to me. "So, Donna, he didn't like your glasses?" I was shocked and amazed at this asshole. Clearly, as if it had just happened, I flashed back to when my attacker opened the car door, dragged me out and broke my glasses. *Has this officer no manners? What is wrong with him? Why is he doing this?*

I finally couldn't take it anymore. "Are you speaking to me?" I asked.

"Oh, so you were listening," he said. "I knew I could get your attention. My friends here and I just wanted to know what you looked like without your glasses on. Could you take them off for us?"

One of the other officers told him to shut up, and he walked away from this jerk, as did the other officer. They knew he was harassing me and didn't want any part of it.

"Who is your sergeant?" I asked him.

My question put him on the defensive, and he told me to find out myself. I couldn't believe this guy. My first reaction was to spray him with a fresh pot of coffee, but I quickly dismissed the idea. I went behind the counter and approached the other officers, asking them who their sergeant was. They were happy to tell me. I made the call and soon the sergeant showed up.

After I explained to the sergeant what happened, he assured me he would talk to this officer and it would never happen again. The sergeant was very cordial and sympathetic. He knew the facts of my case and said he was happy to make my acquaintance. While this was going on, Diana just stood back, wondering what was going on. I never did tell her or anyone. The officer who made the crude remarks never came back in the store, but the sergeant made routine stops to see how I was doing.

Little by little I could feel my confidence building with situations like this. I took the proper action and it worked out for the best. But that incident would not match days to come.

As I was waiting on customers one afternoon, a salesman came in. He put his briefcase on the counter and opened it. Inside were cans of mace, nicely packaged with Velcro straps, all sizes and shapes. He leaned over to me and said, "I heard a young woman working here was murdered and thought it would be a good idea to tell you how this mace might have saved her life."

I looked at him in amazement but allowed him to continue.

"If she would have had this little baby in her hands, she could have escaped the attack and would still be working here probably. This little can is our most popular. It's easy to conceal and easy to handle." He finished his spiel and looked at me expectantly.

I wasn't sure exactly how to react to this, so I just stood there looking at him. Maybe he was right. *Maybe if I had mace that night I could have gotten away. I wish it could have been that simple.* "This is all very interesting," I said.

Diana came over at this point, and he reiterated what he had said to me. She looked at me, then put her arm around me and told him I was the young women of whom he spoke. I thought he was going to lose his teeth.

He stood there with his mouth open for a moment, then stammered, "I-I'm so s-sorry. I heard that you had been murdered. I was given some bad information, and I am really sorry." He closed his briefcase and backed out the door, repeating, "I'm so sorry."

I asked to go home early that day. As soon as I arrived, I ran to my room and cried. I was so confused, questioning myself about my decision and wondering if I would ever go back. Every day was bringing on new challenges. Every day there was an opening of emotional wounds; flashbacks were coming more frequently, more intensely.

The next morning on my way to work I was driving my usual route when I spotted a large, two-story, green, wood-frame house sitting on top of a hill. It was only a minute from the store, but I had not noticed it before. I stopped my car abruptly on the shoulder and stared at this house. I started to shake as day became night and the sounds of cars rushing by me were silenced. I zoned in only on the house: "the house." This was the house to which my attacker had taken me to rape me.

I saw myself running from my attacker and realized how close I was from the major highway. If only I had known and not fallen, I might have made my escape. If only I had run to the left instead of to the right, I would have been on the driveway and out to the highway. I reran the event in my head as I saw myself struggling to escape. If only I had known. If only I had known!

I began trembling, recalling the smell of the army blanket and the mildew smell in his car. This is the house. This is

the house! I saw the house next door; both houses had ve-
hicles parked in the driveways. Suddenly I was extremely
angry no one had come out to help me that night, even though
I had yelled at the top of my lungs.

Now I sat looking at those houses. Time passed...still, I
sat. Finally I retreated to my home, calling my manager and
explaining I was not feeling well enough to come in. I stayed
in my room all day, pacing back and forth, very disturbed.
Once again, I had no one with whom to share my thoughts.
There was no one to listen as I tried to explain how I was
feeling. I thought of Ina, but too much time had passed and I
didn't want to involve her. I didn't want to bother her or
anyone with this.

On my way to work the next day I knew I was approaching the house. This time I would not look. I put up my hand
like a blinder against my face, blocking my peripheral vision.
I made it to work. I was happy to see the many totes of merchandise that were cluttering the aisles. It was grocery day,
and I could work all day filling shelves. It kept me from thinking. Staying busy was my best medicine. I was never
completely free of thoughts, though, as when I would have
to fill the cooler with juice bottles and have a flashback of
my attacker bringing his bottle of juice up to the counter.

The flashbacks occurred frequently. Anything and everything could set them off. A smell, a person, a car, a piece of
merchandise or just standing still. It was becoming harder
and harder for me to concentrate. I would suddenly go into a
trance-like state and stare into the unknown. People would
have conversations with me and I would just stare at them.
Nothing stimulated me. I was a robot doing my job, with no
sense of reality.

It became routine for me to put my hand next to my face
when I drove to work, to avoid seeing the Green House, which
I called it. Pulling into the parking lot at the store one day, I

suddenly felt a rush, a chilling sensation. It wasn't cold out, and I quickly dismissed it. I could see that we would be really busy that particular morning; people were everywhere. I sprinted into the store and moved quickly behind the counter to help my manager with the coffee crowd. We were so busy we couldn't even look up at the customers. We just looked at the merchandise and took the money and said thank you. There must have been 50 people in line. I rushed back and started more coffeepots, then ran over to help Diana. Everything moved quickly. Ring it up…take the money…say thank you. We were a good team, and there was finally a moment when we could look briefly at each other and crack a smile.

As the crowd began to filter out, I noticed a young woman was staring a hole through me. Diana even asked me if I knew her, because the stare was so noticeable. When it came time for the woman to be checked out, I saw that she had a chocolate milk and Tastykake. I remember her so clearly. She was in her twenties, dressed in blue jeans and a white pullover shirt with ruffles around the collar. She just stood there after checking out.

I looked up at her for just a second, then she said, mean-like, "You're the one, aren't you?"

I looked at Diana. Diana looked at me. This woman obviously wanted trouble. I became nervous and didn't want to answer, so Diana did.

"What are you talking about?" Diana asked, still waiting on other customers.

Diana was excellent with people and I felt confident she would take care of this, until the woman leaned over the counter and tried to grab my face to force me to look at her. Diana quickly grabbed her hand and told her to leave.

"You're the one," the woman said louder. Everyone was looking at her.

"Leave! Leave now!" Diana screamed. "I'm going to call the cops."

The woman replied, "Go ahead. Maybe they'll put her in jail for lying." She threw her purchase on the counter.

This situation was becoming violent, and I began shaking. Diana asked me to stand behind her and motioned for the woman to leave.

"I'm not leaving 'til she admits she wasn't raped by Kenneth Morgan," she yelled.

I couldn't believe my ears. The name just echoed in my ears, and I thought I was going to pass out. Imprisoned behind the counter, I started shaking uncontrollably. Diana kept waiting on the few people still in line, yet maintaining her protection over me. The woman waited until the customers were gone and began to come around the counter. Diana picked up the phone and called the police.

"He didn't rape you," the woman persisted. "You had sex with him, didn't you? And then you told the police it was rape. Honey, you are messed up in the head if you think I believe your sick story. He's in jail because of you. You sent an innocent man to jail. How do you feel about that?" Knowing the police would be there any minute, she finally grabbed her purchase from the counter and stalked out.

"Don't you ever return to this store again," Diana yelled at the retreating figure.

Once she was out of the store, I stood unmoving, shocked and catatonic. I was numb, drained, having trouble breathing. Diana helped me off to the back room and sat me down. I was dead inside. I stayed in the back for some time, vaguely hearing voices, wondering if this woman was going to come and finish me off.

I don't know how much time had gone by when Diana came to me. She said the police would press charges if I wanted to. I just mumbled. I couldn't decipher any words or meanings of words. I just wanted to go home—to be safe and away from all of this. Diana was in agreement and offered to take me home, but I don't know how I got home that day.

Several days passed, and I stayed home. Again, I did not tell anyone of my encounter. Genuinely worried and sympathetic, Bill Meyer called me. He had heard what happened and wanted to offer me another position. The minute he made the proposal, I began to think of money. I still needed money. He said he had an auditing position opening up and wanted to offer it to me. Without hesitation, I took the job. He said I would be responsible for auditing 31 stores per month, and I would always have two other people with me; the hours were all during the day. I was pleased. I later found out the woman who ran that department had requested me personally. She later reached the rank of district manager herself.

I never returned to the store.

I started my job without incident, and I enjoyed the hustle and bustle of meeting deadlines and the sense of accomplishment it gave me. It even put more money in my pocket.

Several months passed and I was doing well. I was doing so well, Walter Mantz, a district manager from another zone area, came to interview me for a position in his area. The promotion was for lead auditor, with a raise to boot. I would be out of the corporate stores, in a new area of the county and auditing franchise stores—privately owned stores—still under the umbrella of the corporation and its standards. Instead of 31 stores, this zone had 70. I would have two teams of auditors, and there would be more driving time and more work.

I liked Walter right away. He was a big, burly man—tall, not fat. He was funny and very easy to talk to. This alone was all I needed to make my decision. He was filled with excitement, talking about his district and the people he had working for him. He told me I would be helping with opening new stores and learning other positions. For the first time I was seeing a future. Here was a district manager who believed in me…for whatever reason.

I was in my glory—making money, working hard and learning. All the pieces were falling into place. I worked well with my audit manager, who was as sweet as she could be. We became good friends. I even began going out with her and some others from the district. It was safe and it felt good.

It was early spring when a police officer stopped by my house and served me with a summons for trial. My attacker was pleading "not guilty" to the offense, and I would be the state's star witness. All I had ever been told from the beginning was that he had pled guilty and I would never have to attend trial. This new information threw me into a tailspin. I instantly felt my newly acquired exuberance diminishing.

Now, why now? What in the world is going on? I don't want to deal with this right now. I'm starting my new job and my district manager will flip. I can't screw this up. What do I do? What do I do? What's more important? Why is he pleading "not guilty"? What has happened? He confessed! Now I need to be dragged into this. How can this be happening, now?

So many questions. I could feel my decision-making ability falter. I had no idea which direction to go in. I knew the summons was an important document, and if I didn't show I would be put in jail for failure to appear. I had no one with whom to share this. My mother wasn't sophisticated enough to understand and my father, worthless. Debbie…well, I couldn't burden her, and Barbara was busy with her own business. Both had finally been able to get on with their lives. I noticed the name on the summons under prosecutor and called the state attorney's office in Annapolis. They heard my name and put me right through.

"Hello, Mr. Weathersbee," I said with a shaky voice.

"Yes, Ms. Ferres. Good morning. How are you doing? How can I help you?" he asked over his speakerphone.

"Uh, I just got a summons and want to know what's going on." I blurted.

"Oh, yes. Mr. Morgan has changed his plea, but I want you to know I am on top of this and will take care of everything. I will be meeting with Mr. Morgan's attorney this week and I will keep you updated. Let me just verify the phone number where I can reach you," he said, taking down my number.

"Does this mean I won't have to go to trial?" I asked.

"Well, I can't promise anything. I know what you have been through and I will do everything I can to keep you off the stand. In the meantime, wait for my call. I don't know what's up Mr. Morgan's attorney's sleeve."

Well, God, if you don't know, who does? my mind screamed. You know about as much as anyone else what I've been through, but that isn't saying much. You better get this fucking bastard behind bars and quick. I shouldn't have to go to trial. He admitted the whole thing. I know what his statement said.

"Should I be concerned?" I asked softly, not wanting to know the answer.

"Just hang in there. I'll call you when I speak to him, and I'll get this whole matter straightened out. I'll call you. Try not to worry," he said, clicking off his speakerphone.

With the phone in my hand, I sat for a long time, listening to the loud buzz of the dial tone. I was drained…frozen. Anger turned to thoughts of suicide. There was nothing I could do about this. I couldn't make it go away. I just wanted everything to go away. I wanted so badly to call someone, explain how withdrawn I had become. I needed to be comforted. I just wanted to lie in someone's arms and cry, but I had no one, no one I could trust to see within me, no one to help.

Somehow I made it through those few days on a wing and a prayer. My job didn't suffer as much as I was suffering inside. My sights on the future were fragile and weak, but my physical endurance carried me through. I worked long hours, coming home only to sleep. I had no appetite. I waited patiently for the call back from the assistant state attorney. Finally the call came.

"Hello, Ms. Ferres. This is Frank Weathersbee," he said.

"Hi, Mr. Weathersbee. I've been waiting for your call."

"I spoke with Mr. Harris, the attorney for Mr. Morgan, and together we were able to come to an agreement to keep you off the stand," he said, picking up the handset and taking it off speaker mode.

"Oh, that's great news! So he pled guilty again?" I asked.

"Well it's complicated."

"Complicated? What do you mean?" I asked, sitting down on a kitchen chair.

"Well, you see, in order for me to keep you off the stand, we plea-bargained the sexual assault charge. But we'll still charge him with rape and attempted murder," he added quickly.

"What? What does that mean?" I asked, bewildered.

"It's judicial talk. I had to bargain down the sexual assault to keep you off the stand. Do you understand?"

"No!" I exclaimed. "What is the difference between rape and sexual assault?"

"He'll get rape in the first degree and attempted murder in the first degree. He'll be put away for a long time," Weathersbee assured me.

"But you didn't answer my question," I persisted. "What is the difference between the two?"

"Well, rape is the unlawful act of having sexual intercourse without the female person's consent. Sexual assault is the forcing of the female person to engage in a sexual act by force or threat. So you can see how similar they are. The rape carries much more penalty."

"So would that mean that the charge of holding the knife to my throat and having sex acts with me would be dropped? Don't you understand? If he hadn't had the knife, I might have been able to get away from him. He held me hostage with that knife! Mr. Weathersbee, you cannot do this. You've got to call it all off. He did terrible things to me, and he deserves the harshest penalty. Why would you do that without talking to me?" I yelled.

"I'm sorry you feel that way, Ms. Ferres, but it was something I agreed to do and Mr. Harris is coming over with the final paperwork this afternoon. I am in total agreement with you. He deserves the highest penalty, and I promise you he will get it. The rape and attempted murder both carry life sentences. He will be put away for a very long time." I knew he was anxious to get off the phone.

"I'm coming there to meet with you face-to-face," I declared. "You have to see me and the scars I live with every damn day of my life." I slammed down the receiver without waiting for his response.

I sprinted out to my car, turned the key in the ignition and...remembered I didn't know where I was going. I ran back into the house, called to get directions and rushed out again to jump back in the car. My adrenalin was coursing, and there was nothing going to stop me. Nothing. Annapolis was many miles away. I had been there only a couple of times, but I was determined, and that goes a long way. I don't remember much about the ride, but all of a sudden...there I was.

The building wasn't fancy. I barely glanced at it as I quickly dismissed any qualms about being so far from home and stormed inside. I was going to see Frank Weathersbee and speak my piece. His secretary greeted me.

"Mr. Weathersbee is waiting to see you," she said in a soft, yet firm voice.

I guess everyone expects me, I thought wryly. *With the tone I used on the phone, I'm surprised not to see the place covered in police.*

"Thank you," I said, as she walked me down a short hallway and into his office.

Weathersbee was sitting behind his desk in a leather chair. He stood up and shook my hand. A woman came in behind me, and I was introduced to her. She was Maureen Gillmer, the advocate for the Victims Witness Program. I was glad she was there. We all sat down. Weathersbee was a young man dressed nattily in a blue suit, starched shirt and silk tie. He had a nice face. My anger toward him changed as he began to talk.

"Ms. Ferres, I'm glad you're here," he said. "I'm very pleased to finally meet you. Ms. Gillmer will work with you to get you prepared for any court appearances that may arise. Now, I can understand why you are upset, and I want to make it clear that under no circumstances will Mr. Morgan be freed. What he did to you was a heinous crime and one that he will pay for, for a very long time. I want you to know that."

"Mr. Weathersbee, I may look like I was born yesterday, but I have lived a lifetime since my attack. I am not going to allow any plea bargaining to take place on my behalf. I understand the judicial system and how things fall through the cracks. But I have survived a terrible attack that plagues me daily, and I can't and won't allow it. I will stay here in your office all day explaining to you what my life has been like since my attack. I've had two major surgeries, I'm afraid of my own shadow, and I'm barely able to work. But I am a fighter, and now it is your turn to understand where I stand. I will not drop any charges if I have any say in it. You can't do this to me. You are supposed to be on my side. You've got to reconsider! Please." I began to cry.

Frank Weathersbee glanced over at Maureen and then at me. He put his hands over his face and massaged his eyes with his fingers. He stayed this way for several seconds as he listened to my cries. He took several deep breaths. Maureen pulled a box of Kleenex close to me, but I never took my eyes off him. His obviously strained demeanor showed me some hope that I had gotten through. He finally raised his head and grabbed a file on his desk. He opened it and flipped through its contents. I watched and waited to hear what he would say.

"Well...Ms. Ferres, you are right. I can't with good conscience allow this plea bargain to go through."

Maureen smiled. A long sigh of relief blew from my mouth, emptying all the air in my lungs. "Thank you, sir," was all I could say.

"Ms. Ferres, you do understand now this decision will probably force us into trial. But let me assure you, I will be by your side the entire time, and Mr. Morgan will get what he deserves. Mr. Harris will be by today, and I will tell him what transpired. I will keep Maureen updated, and she will be your contact person from now on." He turned to Maureen. "Now, Maureen, would you take Donna down to the courtroom and show her around? She will need to be aware of what it looks like and where everyone will be seated. Since she's here, let's just do it now. Thank you."

He turned back to me. "Donna, you are a brave young lady. I'm sure I will be seeing you real soon. Take care of yourself." He stood, extending his hand.

Maureen and I left the office. I wanted to jump up and down, but I held it in as I had with other emotions. She took me to her office and introduced me to her staff of volunteers. They all knew me by name and were pleased to meet me.

They talked a little about what had happened in Weathersbee's office, and Maureen filled them in. I stood like a little girl, watching these women express their happiness with the result. I was happy, too.

We walked the long hallway to the elevator and got in to go down two floors. I could feel my heart pounding, and my breathing was labored. I felt as though I was suffocating. As soon as we were off the elevator my breathing returned to normal and my mission to know everything about the trial guided me. The courtroom smelled of fresh wood. All was quiet except for the sounds of Maureen's heels clicking on the wood floor. It took only a few minutes to go through the setup. It didn't do much for me, but I patiently waited until she finished. It just seemed so premature.

We were there for only a few minutes, since I didn't have any questions. She handed me a few brochures and told me to read them. They seemed to cover everything—a map of where the courtrooms were, the seating arrangements and, most important, what the proceedings would involve. On our way back to the entrance of the building I requested that we take the steps instead of the elevator. We did, without question. Maureen explained to me that on the day of the trial she and the other women of the department would be with me. I would not be doing it alone. I thanked her and left.

I returned to work as if nothing were going on in my life. I did my job and I did it well, even though this trial was eating me alive inside. I kept imagining the day I would have to get up on the stand and tell the whole truth of what happened that night. I would have to tell the world about leaving the store! I know how defense attorneys operate. They take a little piece of information and build it against the plaintiff to make their client look good.

And did you smile at him, Ms. Ferres? Did you sit with one leg out of the car? Were you wearing tight jeans? A body-revealing shirt? You knew you were violating store policy when you went outside, didn't you Ms. Ferres? Stop it! Stop it!

The closer the day came, the more I thought of running away. I couldn't even speak to anyone about it, let alone actually do it. The guilt would be out in the open, and I would be the center of attention. How could I allow it?

Two weeks of hell passed. Filled with anxiety, I couldn't sleep or eat. I had convinced myself that what happened was all my fault and the judge would see it that way and let Morgan off the hook. I thought of Morgan's girlfriend, who would probably be in the courtroom, and how she would attack my credibility. I could see the faces of the people in the gallery, Weathersbee and the rape crisis people dropping their chins when they found out the truth—a truth only known to Ina— I had walked outside of my own free will. I was making myself sick. Morgan would be sitting there next to his attorney, laughing at me. This whole thing would be turned around to show it was all my fault. I should never have walked out that door. I felt so weak as I envisioned the defense attorney yelling at me and making me look as though I had wanted this. My mind was working overtime, speculating the worst. Still, I could not share these feelings. If I had done so, I would have to tell the truth.

I wanted so badly to be held by someone and for someone to tell me everything would be all right. In order for me to get what I wanted, I needed to give information. I was not willing to do that. Just a hug, and I would have felt better. I had pushed people so far away from me that the affection I so deeply needed would not enter their minds. I was suffering. I was human. I needed to be hugged and told everything would be all right. Suicide was looking really good to me. I knew I was not going to get support, and it destroyed the self-confidence I had developed since restarting work. My suffering was intense.

I thought of one day—so long, long ago, it seemed—when I was home recuperating from my surgery. I had caught an episode of *Donahue*, in which he was explaining how researchers found that when they put a monkey in a cage without physical touch or companionship, it destroyed the animal's will to live. After years of solitude the monkey died. I remember thinking how cruel the study was, because it touched me deeply. I felt so much sympathy for this poor monkey. I remember I just wanted to love it and hug it all day long. I wanted to rescue it from its cage and show it love without asking for anything in return—just happiness, contact.

I never forgot that monkey, because I believed I was falling into the same category. After so much time of not wanting to be held or touched, that research experiment was extremely real to me. I felt like that monkey. I was scrunched up in the corner, afraid of people, not wanting them to touch me. I had become that poor monkey, and I knew that unless I did something about it, I would be dead. That poor monkey had no choice. He was locked in a cage, not able to reach out and get what he needed. I had a choice; yet I had gone without for so long, I didn't know how to leave my cage or even open the door. I never understood why no one saw it in me, that need—just a hug, a measure of affection without words or explanation. No one, not even my family, knew what I needed so badly.

Early spring brought on more than singing birds, warmth and sunlight. It was a turning point in my life. After many postponements, Morgan finally admitted his guilt and pled guilty. I received the welcome news by mail. As it turned out, no psychiatrist would testify on his behalf. He had tried the insanity defense and the not-guilty defense—all strategies set by his defense attorney. All failed, and he had to plead guilty. Even this, finally, became a strategy.

The
Sentencing

May 5, 1980. Annapolis, the capital of Maryland, sits modestly along the Chesapeake Bay, a traditional Norman Rockwell town with cobblestone streets, historic homes, state office buildings and courthouses, residences of the elite.

Escorting me to the hearing was Brent Williams, the security manager for the convenience store corporate office. I had become close to him over time, and he was someone I trusted. Prior to his position as security manager, he had worked as a homicide detective in Detroit. He explained that he had suffered from "burnout," which ultimately caused him to resign and relocate to Maryland. Williams implemented several new robbery-prevention methods throughout his assigned territory, which was known as the Sunshine District, an area that covered Washington, Virginia and Maryland. These security measures are now used by other, competitive corporations.

Brent was a man with a mission: to prevent crime. We often called him McGruff, the crime dog. His dedication to lowering robbery statistics in his assigned area was by far his biggest challenge. Williams' experience in dealing with criminals guided him to seek out paroled legends of the trade and interview them. Through questioning he had learned, first-hand, why certain stores were targeted. Appetizing attributes for the crooks were low volume, cluttered windows and—topping the list—the amount of money on hand. Each person interviewed admitted he would not take the risk of getting caught for anything less than $50.00. In addition, Williams learned a store robbery should take less than 30 seconds.

Eventually all the stores in the district were conforming to the practice of having less cash in the drawers during peak times, with no more than $15.00 from 11 P.M. to 7 A.M. Brent distributed video training tapes of his interviews with the parolees to all employees on what to do in case of a robbery and how to prevent one. The tapes affirmed money on hand was the motivator and cooperating with the thieves in the event of a robbery saved lives.

Upon reaching our destination at the courthouse, my body stiffened with anticipation. I tried unsuccessfully to reach deep inside myself for strength by taking deep breaths, a relaxation technique I learned through therapy. The deep breaths, however, were now interrupted by flashbacks. Frozen with the fear of seeing my attacker, I sat paralyzed in the passenger seat, momentarily unaware of my surroundings. Suddenly the door opened and Brent's hand appeared. I shook away my paralysis, took his hand and proceeded with him into the courthouse.

We entered through a set of thick wooden doors that led into an atrium with marble floors, a high-peaked skylight ceiling and heavily decorated painted walls. We were greeted by a police guard, who directed us to walk through a door-framed metal detector. A smoked glass billboard permanently affixed to the wall next to the elevators posted the defendants' names and the presiding judges for the numerous courtrooms.

I stood with my back to the wall next to the door of our hearing room, paranoid, fearful of having anyone behind me. The second floor, where we stood, was awash in lawyers, clients, families, staff, witnesses and spectators, all conversing simultaneously and filling the small area with loud chatter that echoed off the walls. Three women from the Rape Crisis Center walked over to me, two of whom I had been introduced to by Maureen Gillmer, the witness advocate, several months earlier. I could see their lips moving, speaking to me, but the amplified chatter all around me drowned out their voices.

Escorted into the courtroom by my supporters, I sat with them in the back row on a wooden bench, awaiting the defendant's arrival. An elderly judge sat on his pulpit bench, looking as if he might fall asleep at any minute. He was hunched over, looking down at some papers in front of him. He could have been asleep, as far as his appearance from where I was sitting. Assistant State Attorney Frank Weathersbee, looking fresh and handsome, turned and nodded, acknowledging my presence. He and I had several meetings before that day, and I was glad he looked back at me. Sitting at the defendant's table was the court-appointed defense attorney, Stephen Harris. Just by glance I could tell he was inundated with cases because of the many files that sat on the table in front of him. I had been told that a public defender had been appointed because Morgan couldn't afford an attorney.

A ruckus at the entrance door announced the presence of the defendant. His chains rang as he was brought in by two armed guards. His eyes immediately gravitated toward the spectator gallery, scrutinizing each individual. As he focused his eyes briefly on me, I gasped. Then he was led to the defense table facing the judge. His shackles were removed.

I felt the warm hand of the crisis worker patting my knee. I stared intently forward, never taking my eyes off Morgan. I could feel my heart rate increase, intensifying my rage, and I felt as if I had just walked into a sauna. Clenching my fists and gritting my teeth, I remembered the person I used to be. I was angry at the thought of the frightened person I had become. For a quick moment I thought of the metal detector and understood why it was needed.

I wanted to scream out, *You son-of-a-bitch, I didn't deserve what you did to me! You piece of slime! You not only tried to kill me for no reason, you stripped me of my self-confidence, my self-esteem and my trust of others. One thing you didn't take from me that night was my will to live, and my determination to keep you behind bars, where you belong. I'm alive, you bastard!* Tears started to fall from my eyes, betraying my anger. I focused again on the hearing.

As the proceedings began, I thought of my family and their reaction when I asked them not to come. I had never told them the truth, a truth with which I was still having trouble. How could I allow them to hear the circumstances of that night, when I still couldn't admit it out loud. After all I had been through and all the support I had been given by family and strangers, I still carried on my shoulders a guilt that would not pass. That guilt presented itself in many ways: refusal to speak of the attack, anger at those who were pressing me for details, rewriting the events in my mind and almost believing it and—most of all—knowing the truth and being afraid to say it.

"Let the court come to order! State verses Kenneth Morgan in the circuit court for Anne Arundel County, Criminal Case No. 22877 and 22892, this day May 5, 1980, before Honorable Matthew Evans."

Weathersbee stood. "State will call at this time State of Maryland verses Kenneth Morgan, Criminals 22877 and 22892 for sentencing.

"Mr. Harris," Judge Evans said.

"Your Honor," responded the defense attorney.

"Is there anything you would like to say in mitigation?" Evans asked Harris.

"Yes, Your Honor, there is," Harris replied. "The remarks I'm about to make to you might attempt to mitigate the crime, Your Honor. We are aware, and my client is aware, of the seriousness of these charges. He, when arrested by police, gave them a full and complete, detailed statement concerning the involvement. And came before this court and pled guilty to the charges of which he stood accused at that time. I would like to call Your Honor's attention, if I might, to several things. One, in the original police report when this incident occurred or shortly after, a caller, at the time unidentified, called the Anne Arundel County Police to inquire about the condition of the victim. At that time he made arrangements with the police to turn himself in. The sergeant in the communications section noticed or indicated during this conversation the subject was crying and seemed to be in a state of depression, when he called. He did, in fact, turn himself in. And when arrested by the police officers who placed him under arrest—I believe, Detective Nauman—he told them he had a history of being a peeping tom and had problems. And his record does not, in fact, bear that out. In my conversation with my client, Your Honor, since meeting him at the Anne Arundel County Detention Center some months ago, there never was an attempt on his part to hide his culpability in this case. We did, in fact, file a written plea of not guilty by reason of insanity. My client said to me at the time he felt he was sick and needed some professional help."

Oh, I remember this day clearly. The day Weathersbee called me to explain this so-called "plea bargaining." What Harris is leaving out here is that their plea for insanity was his bargaining tool with Weathersbee to drop the sexual assault conviction. It almost worked 'til I became involved. Thank God I went in to express my feelings. Only because of my solid reaction, it didn't happen. That is why the plea never went through.

Harris was still talking. "...that as a result of this written plea he was, in fact, sent to Clifton T. Perkins, and they found after examination he was, in fact, sane under the Maryland Law. We come before Your Honor today as a result of guilty pleas to these rather serious...um, not rather, but to these serious charges. I feel my client is asking this Court somehow, for some type of help. The offenses that he stands convicted of at this point—other than a probation before a verdict for tampering with an automobile back in 1972, and 30 days in jail in 1973...well it's unsupervised probation. Thirty days were suspended. Unsupervised probation for destruction of property in 1973. Other than that, this man has no prior involvement with the criminal law. But he stands, according to him and according to the background in the probation report...he had at that time a serious drug and alcohol problem that not only messed up his life insofar as employment, but insofar as being able to have a stable point in his life. He did have a relationship with the girlfriend that is mentioned in this report."

This is absolutely unbelievable. It was his choice to take drugs and drink alcohol. How, in the name of justice for the victim, can he be allowed to claim mitigating circumstances? He was perfectly in sound mind when he attacked me. He knew exactly what he was doing. This bastard took me to his girlfriend's house, where he raped me continuously. Why isn't this being brought up?

Harris hadn't stopped yet. "Since being out of the Anne Arundel County Detention Center, I think it's in his favor to point out the assistant superintendent revealed he is not a disciplinary problem, his attitude and conduct have been excellent, and if the charges against him had been less serious, he would have been considered for a trustee's position."

Where was this attitude and good conduct when I asked him to let me live? Where was this good-natured person who raped me, stood over me and stabbed me over and over again, then left me to die in the woods? Where was this person, of whom he speaks, when he plotted and premeditated my death? Look at your own words, Mr. Harris. Sick, insanity, serious charges, prior offenses and probation. Give me a break.

"His mother, may it please the Court, is present today," Harris was saying. "She has informed me that she was not contacted by the presentence investigator, and she feels that there are certain things in her son's background that she would like to have the Court aware of prior to sentencing. So with the Court's permission I would like to call his mother, please?"

"You may," Judge Evans said.

In the gallery in the front row stood an aged woman. Her large build was covered by an oversized dress, and she walked hunched over to the witness stand. Her slippers dragged the floor as we all watched her turn and look at her son.

"Step right up here, please," the clerk said. "Would you raise your right hand?"

She was sworn in and asked to take a seat. Harris stood before her. "You are the mother of the defendant?"

"Yes."

"Now, in our conversation you advised me that there are certain things in his background that you feel Judge Evans should be aware of. Is this correct?" Harris asked.

"Yes."

"Could you tell His Honor, please, what it is that you feel would help him in passing sentence on your son?"

"Yes. His stepfather repeatedly beat him as a child until he was big enough to get away from him. He was bruised from his neck to his legs many times, three or four times a week. It's caused him problems all of his life."

What about my story? My father, an alcoholic, coming home in the middle of the night, waking me and my sisters and yelling about anything. He used to line us up in the hallway and scream and holler. "Did the dog get fed?" "The house is a mess." One night he didn't like the nightgown my sister was wearing and ripped it off of her. He and my mother would have physical fights, sending my father to jail, and if I intervened I would get thrown across the room. There was never peace in my house. I got a job at sixteen while still trying to stay in school, to help my mother with bills when my father would leave us for long periods of time. My mother had to work the night shift at a factory to keep us from going without, leaving my sister, who was fourteen, to babysit us through the night. That's my story, lady. We all have bruises from our childhood. That's no excuse to try to kill someone.

"What about school?" Harris was asking.

"The schools would call me three or four times a year to come in, beg for him to see a psychiatrist or ask the stepfather to see someone. And it's just his whole life has been like this."

"Were there any tests given to him back in West Virginia where this occurred?"

"It was a school psychologist. They tested him and he'd draw pictures of his stepfather with big fists and his mouth open. They said that most of his emotional problems stemmed from the beatings and the abuse his stepfather gave him."

This line of questioning was almost too much to bear. This poor woman, sitting up on that stand, having to defend her son, a man who had attempted murder. I felt rather sorry for her, knowing by the look of her she didn't have two pennies to rub together. Now her son stood to be convicted of one of the most heinous crimes imaginable. Harris kept at it.

"So what you're indicating to Judge Evans is that there were emotional problems from his background. Is that correct, ma'am?"

"Yes."

"To your knowledge, has your son ever received any psychiatric and/or psychological treatment for these emotional problems?"

"Other than the school's psychologist talking to him?" she asked, seeming confused.

"Well, he dropped out of school," Harris prompted. "Is that correct?"

"Yes."

"And went into the army at that point?"

"Yes."

"And as I understand it, he had some problems while he was in the army, and only stayed there for approximately a year?"

"Yes."

"Is there anything else that you would like to tell His Honor?"

"Yes. About three years ago he called me up about 12 o'clock at night. I met him and we sat all night long. And he told me that he felt like he was very sick and needed a doctor. That he was afraid he was gonna be like his stepfather."

Oh, how sad! One night in all those years, and he makes this confession to his mother. Obviously he didn't get help. He should have gotten help. Does it take attempted murder to get the help you need? It has gone too far. How dare they bring this up? What about all the suffering I've been through? The rape, the stabbing, left for dead? What about my family? I was a working citizen with goals. I've never hurt a soul. What does all this have to do with the crime he is convicted of? Sickness is not a defense in my eyes. I sit here today with scars all over my body, not to forget the emotional trauma I'm still going through. Who will speak for me?

"Witness with you," Harris said, turning and nodding to Weathersbee.

"No questions," Weathersbee said.

"You may step down," Judge Evans said to the woman.

I watched her leave the witness stand, slowly shuffling back to the gallery. Although we had never met, I could feel a sadness about her. I had listened to what she said and wondered why my mother or siblings weren't called to speak. Later I learned victims have no say in the proceedings. No impact statements, not a word about me.

Harris had the floor again. "If Your Honor please, that's basically it. My client has said to me from the first time I met him at the detention center in August that he admitted his participation in this crime. He asked for some type of help. He knows that he needs help."

Help? What about help? Okay, let me get this straight. Let's feel sorry for the criminal. That makes lots of sense. I've been hospitalized twice—once for more than 30 days, the second time for two weeks. Let's talk about help. What about my lost wages? What about my hospital bills? What about my financial obligations—rent, car payment, groceries, gas— the stuff good, working citizens need to take care of themselves? Endless trips to the doctor and therapist. What about that?

The way I see it, I was working to put myself through college and make something of myself. He was driving around on who-knows-what drugs and alcohol, looking for someone to kill so he could get the help he needs. He not only kidnaps me from my employment, but he rapes me in the backyard of his girlfriend's house for who-knows-what sick reason, beats me about my face and body, throws me in his car with my pants tied around my neck, drags me through a wooded area, then stabs me over and over again. He waits 'til he thinks I'm dead, then steals the little money I have in my pocket. What is wrong with this picture? I never had anything given to me as a child or as an adult. Everything I had, I earned myself. Bald tires on my car didn't stop me from going to work everyday. I never called in sick, because I needed the money. I had bills to pay. If anyone needs help, it is me!

"I think his conduct," Harris droned on, "as indicated by the report, since being incarcerated at the Anne Arundel County Detention Center, shows that he's not a behavioral problem while incarcerated. That he has, in fact, furthered his education. He did qualify for his GED examination. And if it were not for missing the time to take the test he would have acquired his GED while in the detention center. Also, since being incarcerated he has become extremely religiously active. He has shown me many certificates for courses that he has completed in religious study from the Washington Bible College as well as the Good News Mission, and the chaplain at the Anne Arundel County Detention Center has given him a letter of recommendation to the fact that he has put his time to good use."

Okay, this is beginning to make sense. I'm dying in the hospital with a respirator breathing for me, tubes up my nose, my kidney is draining into a bag outside my body and he is gathering credits for the Good Samaritan Award. I can hardly sit here and listen to these outrageous remarks. Thank God I have people with me or I think I would explode.

"Again, Your Honor, we are not minimizing the crime," Harris said solemnly. "My client has not asked me to do that. He acknowledges his guilt in this crime. What we are asking, Your Honor, is that he be remanded to Patuxent Institution, where he can get the treatment he needs. If he goes to prison, for whatever period of time it might be, there is going to be a time when he's going to be released. And what we are asking the Court is that the time he's going to spend in prison that he be allowed to use that to acquire some type of help, so that hopefully someday when he returns to the streets he can be a useful citizen and a healthy citizen."

He hasn't even spent time in prison and he's telling the judge, when he gets out, he'll be a productive and healthy citizen! For 28 years of his life, he has not sought any help. Now all at once he is someone's prodigy. He has been given immunity by the state to earn these few pieces of paper over nine months instead of paying for his crime, which any normal human being would think he was doing. Now I hear all this! Outrageous! What about my enrollment in college that I wasn't able to finish because I was in the hospital trying to survive? What about the many certificates I earned for working with disabled children in my spare time? What about the employee-of-the-month certificates I received for never missing a day of work? What about my hopes and goals, taken from me in an instant. These comments are arrogant and lack common sense and reasoning. Is this what really happens to rapists, murderers, kidnapers and convicted felons when they are incarcerated? Oh, heaven help us all. This makes me sick to my stomach.

Frank Weathersbee rose. "Your Honor, it's commendable of defense counsel to not minimize the seriousness of the crime, but I'd like to point out that the Court is well aware of the seriousness of the crime. Had the victim died, and it's very fortunate she didn't, I could imagine this as a case in which the State would have requested the death penalty."

I could feel myself cooling down. All that time I spent with Weathersbee had really done something. Initially he was willing to go with the plea bargain presented by Harris, but I was told about it and made a big commotion. Dropping the sexual assault to get a guilty plea. How absurd! Morgan himself admitted from the beginning that "he had killed the girl at the convenience store," then when given a court-appointed attorney he all of a sudden pled not guilty.

I'm not an attorney, but I know what happened that night and I know who did it to me, I thought. *I picked him out of a photo lineup. No doubt about it. This is a very simple case. How could it have gotten so out of control at the beginning? The death penalty is exactly what he should be given. The fact that he thought he left me for dead is, by Maryland Law, a capital offense, and he should be given the death penalty.*

I was trying to put my life back together from two major surgeries, when all the deals were being made. No one from the state attorney's office ever came to my house to interview me and tell me what was going on. I made the initial call to Weathersbee, and when I found out what the real truth was I drove the 52 miles in my old car, scared out of my mind I would break down, to Annapolis to speak to him in person. If I hadn't been persistent, I would never have had a say in the plea bargaining. If I hadn't interceded, the plea bargaining would have gone through without my knowledge. One of the main reasons I survived, I believe, was my will to catch this bastard and put him in jail. I was absolutely convinced he would do this to someone else.

Weathersbee continued to make his points. "I'd like to point out that in the last several years, of course, the Courts...the Legislature, excuse me, has divided rape into various, separate categories. There are some rapes that properly fit into the category of second degree rape, which has a maximum penalty of 20 years. This is not one of them! This is one of the most aggravated type rape cases that I've seen and, I think, can be imagined, short of the victim's being killed. And, of course, Rape 1 carries a penalty of life imprisonment. I don't know what it was that caused this particular defendant to embark upon this very violent behavior, but as the presentence report indicates, he certainly is an extreme danger to society, and I think the Court should consider the severity of the penalties promulgated by the legislature for this type of activity." Weathersbee returned to his table.

Judge Evans looked toward the defendant's table and commanded, "Stand up!"

Harris turned to Morgan, saying, "Would you stand, please? Now is your opportunity to, if you wish, say what you want to Judge Evans concerning sentencing. This is your right of allocation to say what you want concerning sentencing. You can subtract from, change what I said, add to what I said, or you can remain silent. If you wish to speak to the judge, now is your opportunity."

I looked from side to side at the people who were with me. This was the big moment when I would hear his remorse, the remorse we had heard his defense attorney declare repeatedly. *Now I will hear it from him!*

Morgan stood. "Well, Your Honor, I think everything that ought to be said has been said. And there's nothing I can think of to be extracted. And I'd like to be silent at this time."

I turned and looked at Brent. He raised his eyebrows and shook his head no. I knew what he was thinking because I was thinking the same thing. *No remorse! You coward! Not even an I'm sorry. Just knowing he has been given certificates in Bible Study from the Washington Bible College—and not to forget the Good News Mission and the letter of recommendation from the chaplain from the Anne Arundel County Detention Center—wouldn't one of these teachers have helped discuss what the word remorse means? I would think with all this education in religion he would know that taking responsibility for his actions would set him free. All that talk about religion was just a smokescreen to sway the judge to feel sorry for this lowlife. Well, it isn't going to work with me. If he truly felt it, he would have said it.*

Maybe the judge was thinking the same thing. He asked, "Is there anything else?"

"No, sir," the defendant replied.

"Would you two counsel approach the bench?" the judge asked. I couldn't hear the bench conference, but it was recorded in the court documents. Evans said, "I just want you to refresh my memory. This law was changed. The rape, that's life. First degree is life, too, isn't it?"

Weathersbee replied, "Yes, sir."

"It's rape in the first degree?" Harris asked.

"Yeah," Evans said.

"Rape in the first degree and sexual offense in the first degree," Weathersbee reminded him.

"Right," Evans said.

"They're both life," Weathersbee repeated. "Kidnaping is 30 years, assault with intent to murder is 30 years."

"Thirty years," Evans echoed.

"And, of course, the other in the case, robbery, is 10 years," Weathersbee persisted.

"Ten, yeah. I just wanted to be sure I had it right," Evans said. "Thank you."

The suspense was killing me. Morgan sat staring at the table in front of him. I could see Judge Evans scratching his head at times and Harris looking down at the floor. I could only surmise things were going well for me. I turned and looked at my supporters and anxiously smiled, as we awaited the sentence.

"What could be taking so long?" I asked Brent in a whisper.

"They're probably just sorting out the sentence before it goes on record," he whispered back.

We all took one another's hand in a type of vigil. I looked up in front of me where Morgan's mother was. I could only see the back of her head.

After what seemed an eternity, the conference broke up and the attorneys returned to their tables. As the judge rustled some papers in front of him and was about to speak, I held my breath and tightened my grip on the hands of those beside me.

Judge Evans cleared his throat. "Let's see. Kenneth Morgan, would you please stand? In case Number 22877 Criminals, versus the State of Maryland, it's the judgment and sentence of this Court as to count 1, that you be committed to the jurisdiction of the Commissioner of Correction for the term of your natural life.

"And as to count number 3, it's the judgment and sentence of this Court that you be committed to the custody and jurisdiction of the Commissioner of Correction for the term of your natural life. And this sentence is to run concurrently with the sentence imposed in count number 1. In count number 5, it's the judgment and sentence of this Court that you be committed to the custody and the jurisdiction of the Commissioner of Correction for a term of 10 years. And this sentence is to run concurrently with the sentence imposed in count number 1 and count number 3.

"As to count number 6, it's the judgment and sentence of this Court that you be committed to the custody and the jurisdiction of the Commissioner of Correction for a period of 10 years. And this sentence is to run concurrently with the sentences imposed in counts number 1, 3, and 5.

"Third count, the robbery count. It's the judgment and the sentence of this Court that you be committed to the custody and the jurisdiction of the Commissioner of Correction for a period of 10 years. And this sentence to run concurrently with the sentence imposed in 22877 Criminals.

"I further have to advise you of certain rights that you have as a result of these sentences being imposed. You have a period of 30 days from today to enter an appeal to the Court of Appeals. And if you do enter an appeal you have within 10 days to order from the court reporter a transcript of the proceedings in these cases. You also have a period of three days in which to file a motion for a new trial. You also have the right to file a Petition for a Review of Sentencing by a panel of three judges. And I would not be a member of that panel. And they would have the…listen carefully, now…if you did file this, they have the right to increase or decrease your sentence. And you also have a period of 90 days from today in which to file a Petition for a Modification of Sentence. And that petition would be heard by me. Do you have any questions?"

I leaned over and whispered in Brent's ear. "What does all this mean?"

"It means he is going away for a very long time. He has been given two life terms plus 30 years. Unfortunately, the judge has ruled to run concurrently," Brent replied, looking straight into my eyes. This is what I liked about Brent. He never pulled any punches. He made good eye contact and stuck straight to the facts.

"What do you mean, 'unfortunately to run concurrently'?" I asked.

"Donna, it means all the sentences will run together, as if he had only received one life sentence," Brent explained. "And because of this, he will be eligible for parole by Maryland's law in 12 years. If the judge had considered it consecutive terms, then Morgan would serve one life term, then start another life term, then start the other. He wouldn't have been eligible for parole 'til he was in his sixties. Still, I feel it is a good starting point."

I saw that Harris had taken the floor again. "If Your Honor, please, my client has been incarcerated on this charge since August the fourth, 1979."

"Well, these sentences then will modify to start as of what date?" Evans asked.

"August 4, 1979," Harris replied.

"August 4, 1979, and that would be in each case," Evans announced.

"Your Honor, please, there's one further thing," Harris said. "Would Your Honor refer my client to the Patuxent Institution for an evaluation?"

"Yes," the judge replied.

"I thank you very much."

The judge acknowledged Harris's comment, excused Weathersbee at his request, then declared the court adjourned.

As Weathersbee made his way out of the courtroom he looked over at me and smiled. I smiled back and shook my head in agreement. We sat still and watched as the armed guards cuffed and shackled Morgan, who did not even glance toward his mother as he was escorted out of the room. I looked briefly at his mother, who was all alone in the front row. I felt bad for her.

"Well, it's over." I said, addressing my supporters. "Thank you all very much for being here. I don't think I could have gone through it without you. I'm sure a celebration is in order, and I do know this, he will not be out on the streets to hurt anyone for a long time. This is a good thing," I said, shaking everyone's hand.

Leaving the courthouse I remember thinking to myself, *After all that was said today, not one person here could imagine the truth and what really happened.*

That night, safe in my bed, I fell asleep quickly, assured Kenneth Morgan could not touch me for at least 12 years. At 3:04 A.M. my eyes flew open, and I was hurled back nine months, to the wee hours of August 3, 1979.

10 Flashback!

It's the quiet time now at work...my day off, covering for another employee who's sick. I don't mind, because I enjoy the extra pay and I'm gaining experience toward my management career. And I like the midnight shift. It gives me the freedom to work at my own pace, meet new people, and do a spit-and-polish cleanup, working toward winning the best-looking store award. As usual, I have made a cursory walk around the store to see what needed to be done. As usual, the merchandise on the shelves was in disarray, a pet peeve of mine. Fronting the merchandise on the shelves makes for a well-stocked and organized appearance, a task that, when completed, is self-satisfying.

Volume is usually hit and miss before the bars close at 2 A.M., then busy 'til 3, then slow. Like clockwork the paper carrier comes in around 3:15 to drop off the various racing forms and multiple newspapers. People wait in their cars outside the store for the drop-off. They inevitably have them read before paying for them. Two of them are women who come in often. They have explained to me the gambling logic behind horse racing betting, and we joke about it tonight. I never go for it, but they enjoy talking to me about it.

As the two women leave, the last of the small crowd, I notice one car still in the parking lot. Alarmed, I open my cash drawer and make a money drop of bills into the safe, leaving me only the amount emphasized by company policy of $15.00 after midnight. I can't see into the car, but it's obvious someone is there. Hesitant to leave the confines of the counter area, I stay near the phone, keeping one eye on the vehicle. This isn't normal. Maybe I should have an officer drive by. No, that's silly. It's probably just someone sleeping or resting. If something's on his mind, he sure isn't acting on it.

I continue my routine, keeping an eye on the door. It's about 3:30 now. I'm swabbing the floor when I hear a car door close. I look out the front window, but due to the glare of the inside lights, I can only see a figure walking toward the store. I quickly lean the mop, still in its bucket, and walk behind the counter toward the phone. I wait.

The buzzer on the door sounds and the man, wearing jeans and old army coat, walks in with his head dropped, heading toward the cooler area. I yell out hello, but there is no response. He stands facing the cooler windows for minutes until he finally decides on a fruit drink. I never take my eyes from him. As he begins to walk closer toward me, his head still lowered, I notice that I might know this guy. Somewhat relieved, I greet him again. Now at the counter, he looks up at me. Treating him like any other customer, I try to sell a fresh donut.

"No, thanks," he says. Reaching his oil-stained hand into his unwashed jeans pocket, he spills change on the counter and tells me to take what I need. I count it and slide some back to him. He picks up the change and turns to leave. Almost out the door he turns. "Aren't you Debbie's sister?"

"Yes, I am," I say with a smile on my face.

"How is she doing? I haven't seen her in a long time," he says, walking back toward me.

"She is doing terrific. Thanks for asking. What are you doing out so late on a work night?" I ask, prompting a conversation, not knowing how well he knows my sister. He seems friendly enough, although there is a strangeness about him.

"I figured since I stayed up this late, I might as well just stay up 'til I go to work," he says softly. I can smell a faint odor of alcohol on his breath. "I've been sitting in my car trying to close my eyes, but I can't seem to sleep," he continues, "and when I tried to start my car to leave, my car wouldn't start."

"Hmmm…you know, there is someone I can call who is open all night that will come and help you with your car," I say. "His number is right here." I reach under the phone for the number.

"No, that won't be necessary," he replies. "I know what's wrong. The points in my carburetor are touching, but I can't seem to do two things at once. I just need someone to jolt the ignition while I reset the points. No big deal, really. I don't have the money to pay someone for a five-second job." For the first time, he makes sustained eye contact.

I hesitate. "I can't help you," I say, "sorry. I have to stay in the store. It's policy."

"Okay. I'll try and do it myself. Maybe someone will come by."

"Take care of yourself," I say as he leaves the store. I watch him as he walks out to his car and raises the hood. I return to mopping. Halfway through the store with my mop and bucket I hear the buzzer go off. I look up and see it's the same guy. I pull the bucket up to the counter and again retreat behind it.

"I really could use your help. It will only take a minute. I'm sure you have a minute for an old friend of your sister," he says.

I look at him and think, *The sooner I get this guy on his way, the sooner I can finish my work.* "Okay," I say, relenting. "What do you need me to do?" I walk out behind him.

He opens the door to the driver's side. "Just sit inside. As soon as I give you the word, jolt the ignition."

The car reeks of mildew and sweat as I sit awaiting instruction. It is an old Nova, one year older than the one I drive, but blue. I've been familiar with cars since I was a kid. My old friend, Michael, a car junkie, taught me everything— from oil changes and tune-ups, to carburetors, changing flat tires, electronics, pistons, cylinders…everything. I'm familiar with the problem with this car, and I'm glad to help. It brings back memories of Michael and me.

I've lost track of time, sitting and remembering Michael, looking at the mess inside the car. The car door is open but the inside light isn't on, allowing me a clear view of the parking lot. Suddenly antsy over the long wait, I peer through the crack of the open door to see what the holdup is, thinking I could have this done by now. Suddenly a queasy feeling hits my stomach. He isn't looking under the hood at all. No. He's scanning the surroundings. I'm sitting here daydreaming and something isn't right! I jump from the car, sprinting around the rear of the vehicle and making a mad dash to the door of the store.

Only a few feet from the entrance door he grabs me from behind, forcefully pressing a knife to my throat and penetrating a layer of skin. Flopping like a fish out of water to loosen his grip on me, I clench my right hand around the single-edged knife and scream at the top of my lungs, "Let me go." With all my strength I lift my foot into the air and jam my heel into his upper thigh, disabling him for a moment as I plan my next move. My mind is racing, frantically searching for ideas about how to get away. I am powerless against his brute strength, but my mind is strong. I know as long as I keep my hand around the knife, he cannot slice my throat.

Everything is happening so quickly. *Why doesn't someone drive into the parking lot?* I can see cars going up and down the highway 200 feet away, but nobody can see me struggling. My screams are so loud, surely I can get the attention of someone, especially the firemen across the street. They must be awake; they always visit me during the night.

He becomes a violent, madman. He jerks the hold I have on the knife, causing a deep laceration to my pinky finger. Blood spurts everywhere. He puts the knife back on my throat and throws me into the car. Spinning his tires from the parking lot, he immediately pulls out his penis and forces me down on his lap. I refuse to do what he wants, causing him to stop the vehicle and push me down. I won't do it! *Oh my God, I've got to get the hell out of this car.* He keeps my head down on his lap. I ease my foot over and lift the doorhandle to the passenger door, causing it to open. I jerk away and flip over, going face-first toward the open door. He hits his brakes, causing me to fall backward into the car. I am captured once more. Not one soul is out tonight! I scream and scream, but no one hears me.

With his right arm he puts me in a headlock as we start back down the road. I am getting weaker and weaker. Nothing I try is working. I am so scared! We're bumping down a road…now we stop in a parking area between two houses. He rips my glasses off my face and breaks them in half, throwing them in the backseat. He pulls me from the car, and again I feel the opportunity to escape. Surely I can awaken someone in one of these houses. My mind is working overtime on an escape plan. I have to get away from this maniac!

He has evil in his eyes as he rips my pants off and ties them around my neck, then drags me along the ground behind one of the houses. I scream and scream, "Help me! Help me!" Not a light comes on in either house, nor does anyone come out to discover what all the noise is. He punches me flat in my mouth and warns me that if I pull another stunt like that he will kill me. I am bleeding from my nose and mouth. He tears off my clothes and rapes me, keeping the knife at my throat the entire time.

He tries kissing me, but each time I quickly turn my head in disgust. My mind is beginning to detach from the situation, leaving only my body for him to abuse. Finally...finally, he stops.

"Please," I say, "please...I have a child at home that really needs her mommy. Please let me go. I promise to not speak a word of any of this."

He looks at me with evil eyes and tells me to shut up. At one point he reaches for something away from me, giving me an opening. I jump up and run, but I fall into a hole and lose my balance; he grabs me again. He picks me up and slams me against one of the houses, punching me again and again in the face. Silently I collapse, pretending to be unconscious. Without hesitation he picks me up by my hair and keeps smacking me in the face until I open my eyes. I scream loudly now, so close to this house, but still no one comes.

He drags me by the pants, still attached around my neck, back to the car. He opens the trunk of the car. *This will be my coffin*, I think. He pulls an old mildewed army blanket from the trunk, lays it on the ground, throws me on top of it and begins raping me again. My face is so swollen and sore I can't fight anymore. I don't want to be hit again. I am exhausted and beaten down. He wins. I have no other means of escape; I know I am going to be killed.

Now he is throwing me back into the car. He starts driving. My panties are still around my ankles and, slowly, I reach down and pull them up. He glances my way and smirks. I feel so dirty, but pulling up my underwear gives me a sense of decency. A few minutes later the car stops again. A large mud puddle prevents the car from going any further. He pulls me out of the car by my pants, and I fall to the ground. I refuse to walk to my death. He drags me through the puddle of water and over a rocky, sandy pathway. I am choking from his grip, but I know I can't save myself. He starts yelling to me to stand up, but I won't. I know it is hard for him to pull me; it is my last resistance.

He stops, looks down at me and tells me he is taking me to a shed where he will keep me until he decides what to do with me. A shed! I can escape from a shed. I can't see a shed, but my eyes are swollen and I have no glasses. I believe him and stand up, ready to walk to a place from which there is hope of escape.

I follow for a short distance, then he tells me to walk in front of him. As I walk ahead, he throws me down and punches the knife into my chest. I grunt from the impact and double up as I roll over. He punches the knife twice more into my back. I curl into a fetal position and don't move, not one inch. He puts his face down to mine to see if I am breathing. I don't move one muscle. He begins kicking me around. How do I know to do this? I allow my body to be limp and give the impression I am dead.

Because of my positioning and lack of sight, I'm not sure what he is doing now. Where is he? I don't know how bad my wounds are. I can feel the blood running down my side and legs, but I am managing to breathe softly without his knowing. As I lie here, my hearing becomes acute. I can hear him walking back and forth around my body for what seems an eternity. I hear him walk toward me, then away. Toward me and then away. Then around me. Now I don't hear him at all. Suddenly he hits me over the head with a board. I do not make a sound, although it hurts tremendously. He kicks me over and over again. I don't make a sound. Now the walking around me starts again.

I don't know how much time has passed. Where is he? I don't hear him. Is he playing a game? I lie here. Waiting. Waiting. I do not hear the car start or any sound of his leaving. Slowly into my consciousness comes the sound of a dog barking. I must have passed out.

The dog is barking. *Is this a trick? Should I get up?* Oh my God, what a decision I have to make. *If I get up and he is still there, I will surely die at his hand.* The longer I contemplate my decision, the louder the dog barks. I dig deep into my soul. I must do something. I can't allow my family to go through my death. I don't want them to have to take care of my debts. I concentrate on my family and the trauma they will endure if I die here. Closing my eyes, I ask God what I should do. The dog's barking echoes in reply. That is my answer.

Slowly, gingerly, I stand up. Just the noise of doing that scares the living daylights out of me. Quickly I look around, although without my glasses and with the sand that has been ground into my eyes, I can barely see. No one is here, but phantom footsteps play havoc in my mind. Again I hear the dog and begin walking toward the sound. Ahead of me lies a wooded area, and I can see a faint light beyond it. As I start walking toward the woods, dried leaves beneath my feet create an uproar to my ears. I run into sticker bushes! I can't get around them, so I have to go through them, pushing through them with my body.

Constantly I turn, fearful he is right behind me, ready to kill me. With superhuman force I push myself through the stickers, breaking them with my bruised and battered body. I push ahead hard until…Oh, God, a dead tree lying across my path. I can't get around it, and going back is impossible. I have to move the tree. How can I? Somehow I pick it up, duck under, let it fall, gasping in terror when it falls back in place with a loud, crackling sound. The dog barks more intensely now, so I know I am close to civilization and survival.

Finally I come out on the other side of the woods. All I have to do now is cross this small residential road and make it to the house where the dog is. Will he be sitting at the corner, waiting for me? Again I question God for the answer. The dog barks. I run as hard as I can toward the house. Crying in terror, I knock on the front door until a light comes on. Someone peeks out the window.

"Please!" I call. "I've been stabbed, and I need an ambulance."

There is no response, except for the light going out in the house. I am left standing there, dying. I lay my head on the doorbell with the little strength I have left. The bell rings, rings, rings. I keep my head on the bell. By God, if they won't help me, they will listen to the doorbell ring until I die.

A man hollers through the door, instructing me to go around the house and sit on his porch. I walk around and...Jesus, the porch is on the second floor! I see those steps and think, *I can never make my way up there*. But I do it. Okay. I need to get out of view from the road anyway. This is good. I sit in a lawn chair at the top of the stairs. A man and woman appearing stooped and frail—elderly—stand inside the sliding glass doors, staring at me. They tell me through the glass they have called an ambulance. I thank them and ask for a drink of water. They place the glass of water outside the glass door, onto the porch, then quickly slide the door shut again. I must look awful...scary. They're afraid of me, this bloody mess of a human being wearing only a pair of panties.

The police arrive first. I know some of them, from the store. They line the porch, looking down at me with such sadness. I begin to tell them what has happened; one officer kneels next to me and takes my hand. As soon as I tell them the location of the rape, two officers rush off to investigate. The others stay. With the ambulance siren sounding now in the distance, I look each officer in the eye as best I can.

"Get that son-of-bitch and shoot him for what he did to me," I say with all the strength I have left. There are murmurs of agreement all around.

The paramedics run up onto the porch. My friend Calvin kneels next to me and immediately begins an IV. He surveys my wounds and covers them with gauze pads.

"Listen to me, Donna," he says. "I'm going to get you to the best hospital with the best equipment. I've called for a helicopter."

I thank him and begin to cry. He is a man, but his manner is warm and soothing. He takes my vitals and writes them down, then yells down to the other paramedics to get that helicopter here. Now! I know I'm in trouble. I have never seen Calvin so serious. I know this is serious. He runs down to the ambulance and brings a blanket to me.

As they are loading me into the helicopter, one of the police officers returns, swerving into the driveway and insisting on talking to me before I leave.

"Donna, we found a wallet. We're going to nail this guy! Now you do what you need to do to stay alive, and we'll get this S.O.B. for you," he says, compassion resonating in his voice. "Take care."

I am relieved to know this. If I don't make it, they'll get the guy who did this to me. As they lift me into the helicopter, a young paramedic comes to my side and with tears in his eyes says, "We will all be praying for you." I turn and give a quick look over my shoulder to see all those men watching my exit.

I shake myself, struggling out of the memory. *Well, they got him,* I say to myself. *I'm alive and they got him. He's in jail, and I'm ready to get on with my life.*

11 Moving On

It was clear everyone in my life was ready for me to move on. The sentencing was over, Morgan had been sent to prison and I was free to get on with my life. "Less is more" were the words I spoke every morning before heading out. Ina's advice stayed with me, and I tried to live by those special words that meant to me, don't rush the healing process. Even though to others the trial was over and things seemed to appear normal, I still struggled.

I eventually moved out from under my sister's wing to live in a county closer to work. Shortly after my attack I had met a woman who was doing her medical school training at the hospital in which I spent so much time for complications from surgery. It so happened Roxann had to leave her apartment for six weeks to complete her education before receiving her medical diploma. She knew I was making the long drive to work every day, some 30 miles each way, and she asked me to move in and care for her apartment until she returned. Her apartment was only minutes from my district, and a change of venue was exactly what I needed. I moved in right away.

Roxann was an exceptionally liked and respected person. She touched people with unconditional affection and knowledge. She was a worldly person, too, with stories of France, Europe and the Galapagos Islands. I enjoyed her company so much because she taught me a lot, and I liked her many funny stories. I felt completely at ease with her. She was one of those people you knew, right from the beginning, you could trust.

Living alone in the apartment was somewhat unnerving at times, especially since the laundry room was in the basement area. I was so frightened to go down there I held off doing my laundry until the very last minute. The reason was because there was no escape route. Once I was inside the room, I was trapped. The door never wanted to stay open on its own, and I would literally have to hold the door with my foot while I did my laundry. I needed to be close to the door at all times.

Each time I would hear someone walking down the stairs, I would stop what I was doing and run out of the room, leaving everything. Once the coast was clear I would begin again. Laundry took a long time to do, since I was always looking over my shoulder, and my nervousness made for mistakes. I got to know some of my neighbors going in and out of the building, but still the thought of being alone with any of them in the laundry room was a fear I never overcame. Every stranger was a potential attacker. Male, female, young, old, black or white, it didn't matter.

Everything I did outside the apartment and work was rushed—taking out the trash, doing laundry or just going to my car. When I returned home from the grocery store I would use all my strength to carry all the bags in together, thus avoiding a second trip outside. The less time I spent out in the open, the better. I was constantly afraid.

My new position at work was good therapy for me. I worked well with my peers. Walter Mantz was always looking out for me, stopping to talk to me when he would see me alone. He would tell me how pleased he was with my work. I was so glad to hear these words, yet wondered what his motive was. I truly hoped he was sincere.

The more he would compliment me, the harder I worked. I implemented charts and scales that assisted the field representatives to oversee their stores' inventory problems. It became a tool they relied on. Further, I charted all 70 stores for my district manager. He was so pleased with this information he took it to the zone manager, and it became an intricate part of my job. Soon I had all the management people calling me and asking me questions regarding their stores.

Inventory was a vital part of their jobs, and the more information and better understanding they had, the better they could explain inventory problems at chart meetings, which were held once a month. This was their opportunity to stand before their bosses and explain their profits and losses for that month. I understood these chart meetings to be very intense. I had heard that one field rep was standing at the podium giving her store's information when she was interrupted by the zone manager, who could be really tough. He asked her a series of questions without giving her time to answer, and she fainted from the stress. She fell over the podium and onto the floor. This was how stressful these meetings could get. I heard if you didn't have all the answers, you'd better be a good liar. I didn't know the zone manager too well, but later he and I would be at odds.

Late in 1980 I developed physical pain that affected my job. I couldn't lean over or lift anything without discomfort. A doctor's appointment confirmed I was suffering from kidney stones and adhesions, causing a bowel obstruction in my small intestine. I needed surgery. I immediately called my district manager. He understood and told me to take all the time I needed to get better.

The last thing I wanted to do was have this surgery, but I knew there was no alternative. I went to my mother's apartment to tell her about it, dreading what she would say. She was tired of my illness, weary of my inability to get on with my life, and on this particular day she was not in the right state of mind for any news like this. She was in a bad mood. Even though I was walking bent over, she never tuned into my problem. I was hoping she would open the door for conversation, but it never happened. I was scheduled to go into the hospital the next day, so I had to tell her. Finally I just blurted it out. She didn't handle it very well. I started crying at her lack of compassion for me, and this didn't help matters.

Suddenly she started pulling books from the bookshelf, glancing at the titles and throwing them on the floor. Finally she picked up one, looked at the title in satisfaction and slammed it down on the coffee table. "You don't need surgery for kidney stones!" she screamed at me. "Look! It says it right here." She flipped through the pages and poked her finger down. The book was dated sometime around 1960.

I tried to explain to her it was much more than the kidney stones that necessitated the surgery, but she continued to defend the book's explanation. She was a madwoman. Eventually the conversation got so heated on her side, she picked me up from the couch and threw me against the wall. Immediately, a flashback to the attack slashed across my mind. I ran for the door without grabbing my coat. I ran as hard as I could to my car, then remembered my keys were in my coat pocket. I would have to return to my mother's apartment. All of a sudden I realized I was outside. It was dark, and I was vulnerable. I didn't want to go back. I just stood outside in panic.

Trembling, I crept back to my mother's door. My little brother, who had seen the whole incident, had my coat waiting for me. I was so angry I cried all the way home. *How could she do this to me? I have to have surgery tomorrow. What in God's name was she thinking, throwing me against the wall like that? For God's sake, woman, are you nuts? I'm your daughter. I came to you in person because I didn't want to tell you over the phone. I drove 30 miles in the dark to tell you this and you assault me? I have had enough. Enough!*

By this time Roxann was back, having invited me to continue to live at her house. She was home when I got there, and she could see how upset I was. I couldn't even talk about it. Who in their right mind would believe this had happened? It wasn't until a few days after my surgery that I told Roxann, because she was wondering why my mother never came to the hospital.

After seven days of an NG tube, needles, IVs and stitches that would leave a scar from my chest bone down below my bellybutton, crisscrossing my previous scar, I was sent home. I was so angry at my mother, not only for what she did, but because she never called the hospital to see how I was doing. Even my district manager sent me flowers. I was so happy to have Roxann as my friend. No matter what, I knew I could count on her.

After being home for only two days I began vomiting. I couldn't hold anything down in my stomach. I was dehydrated and weak. When my color changed from a pinkish tone to sand-like, Roxann took me immediately to the emergency room. I had developed another bowel obstruction and was admitted. After several x-rays the obstruction was found to be in my small intestine. My doctor told me in cases like this surgery could be put on hold while they tried a more conservative approach. Because I had just had surgery, the doctor didn't want to reopen the incision unless absolutely necessary.

I was admitted and placed in the cardiac unit, the only bed available. I was doubled over by intermittent, sharp stomach pains so intense I screamed aloud. Into my room walked a black man about 6 feet tall wearing a white doctor's coat. In his hand was a plastic bag with a long tube in it. I instantly had a flashback of Dr. Karmi's trying to put those tubes in my ureter. "What are you going to do with that?" I asked with a gasp.

"Hello, Ms. Ferres. My name is Dr. Jeanne-Pierre," he said with a Creole accent.

"Hello, Doctor. What are you going to do with that?" I repeated.

"Now, now, don't worry. This will only take a moment to insert, then you will feel much better. You can trust me. I have done these many times." He put on surgical gloves and tore open the plastic bag. He didn't call in a nurse or anything.

When he uncoiled a 36-inch white hose from the bag, I thought for sure I was going to pass out. I could instantly feel perspiration under my arms and on my hands.

"Now, Ms. Ferres I need you to hold still. I know this looks bad, but it will only take a moment." He grabbed the end of the tube with a two-inch balloon on the end, and he began to stuff it up my nose.

I jerked my head away. "Do you honestly think I'm going to allow you to put that thing up my nose while I am awake? I demand to be asleep. Put me out. Please! I've been through this before, and it is not pleasant." I could feel my eyes bulging they were so wide open.

"Have you had this before?" he asked.

"Well, not exactly that, but worse," I replied. Every 10 seconds I was doubling over with pain.

"We must do this now," he insisted. "I need to do this to help stop that pain you're having. Now, sit back. As you can see this end has a balloon on it. It is filled with mercury, so it will move down quickly to the stomach and into the intestinal area. This first part will be the most uncomfortable. Are you ready?" He stood face-to-face with me. He was a big man, with big fingers and a big nose.

I had to try to control, not only my pain, but also my emotions as this man lay almost on me. "Yes," I said, taking a deep breath.

He pushed the mercury balloon into my right nostril with his forefinger, but it wouldn't go. The balloon was as round as a quarter and as thick as a golf ball. Next thing I saw was him grabbing a 5-inch Q-tip.

"You've got to be kidding me!" I yelled.

"You will see, Ms. Ferres. This works very well. I will be very gentle. Head back," he commanded, leaning over me.

Oh, my God. How in the world is he going to put that huge thing down my nose? I can't believe this is happening to me again. It hurts. It hurts. Stop! I can't. Stop, please.

"Ms. Ferres, here is a glass of water. As soon as I start pushing, drink this water. It will allow the balloon to go down without choking you. I have it almost in…now! Start drinking." He pushed the contents through the small opening of my nose. "It's through. We did it," he said. My nose started to bleed all over his glove. "Don't worry about that. It will stop. Now I must push the rest of this tube through. The hard part is done," he declared, pushing the tube through as if he were feeding a cable line.

"How long before I start feeling better?" I questioned.

"What we are hoping is that when the balloon makes it to the obstruction, it will penetrate through and open the passage. This may take some time. I will make sure you are given plenty of medication to help you with the pain you are having," he promised, winding down the last few feet of the tube.

I spent the next 10 days in the hospital with that long tube. I didn't eat for almost two weeks. To make the situation worse, my room was right across from the kitchen, and after a few days I began to feel better and was getting very hungry. I was absolutely miserable. I asked Roxann to call my sisters and tell them not to come visit because I was feeling so bad. She did as I asked.

One day while I was sleeping comfortably in my hospital bed, my mother walked in as though nothing had happened. I hadn't seen or spoken to her since her attack on me. My first reaction was pleasure until I remembered that night. I couldn't speak because of the tube in my throat. She came over to me—no kiss no hug—and saw a little blood in the plastic container that held the contents of my stomach matter; she began demanding a doctor. She was yelling up and down the hall. I couldn't believe my ears. I wanted to get out of bed to make her stop, as she continued. I was so embarrassed. Roxann came walking in and asked me what was going on. I couldn't speak, but she knew something wasn't right with me. That's when my mother came walking back in with a doctor.

This was a doctor I had never seen before. She showed him the container and he quickly explained that the tube was brushing up against my stomach lining, which caused the small beads of blood. My mother was not satisfied and continued to make a scene. Roxann finally stepped in and told her I was fine. My mother didn't want to hear anything. She had her mind made up, and she was going to continue to act out. After a few minutes of this I sat up with the little strength I had and pointed to the door. I screamed with my hoarse voice, "Out! Out!"

Oh, my God. Why is she doing this to me? What could be going through her mind? If this is how you treat a sick person, I don't want anything to do with you. Get out! Get the hell out!

My mother got the message because she immediately left the room. I began to cry, causing a clump of sinus phlegm to fill my throat. I couldn't swallow it because of the long NG tube, so I threw it up. And I kept throwing up. I couldn't stop crying. My mother had hurt me so badly. I just wanted to scream.

Why was this happening to me? What did I do that was so terrible to deserve this? Whose mother would do such a thing? She hates me for what I've been through. I can't help it. It happened. I can't make it go away.

Roxann stayed with me until my pain medication took affect. For once in my life I had someone I could rely on and who would stand by me, no matter what. I got from her the very thing I had been looking to find in others, but no one else knew how to give it. I was lucky to have her in my life. My mother didn't speak to me for the next year and a half after that. She refused all my phone calls and wrote "Return to Sender" on any cards I sent to her.

I returned to work six weeks after that surgery. I continued to do well, and my will to succeed grew. It was about the middle of 1981 when a job opening became available for zone audit manager. I wanted it badly. Even though my self-confidence could have used a lot of work, I went to my district manager to tell him I was throwing my hat into the ring. As always he was very supportive of my decision and said he would do whatever I needed to help me. I then went around to get feedback from the field representatives, whom I had come to know very well. Everyone told me to submit my résumé and go for it. All said they would support me.

I submitted my résumé and an appointment was made for me to meet with Rod Cameron, the zone manager, the same man who had caused someone to faint at a chart meeting, the same man everyone feared. I was scared too, but Roxann helped me to prepare. We did role-playing and I took notes. Most of all she convinced me I was as good as anyone to do this job.

I walked into Cameron's office wearing a navy blue suit and silk shirt. I was looking and feeling good about myself. He cordially asked me to sit down. I had with me a briefcase filled with papers to which I frequently referred as my "I am good" file. He gave me latitude to present my work and listened patiently. I smiled frequently, believing things were going well. I knew Walter Mantz and several field reps from my district, as well as other districts, had spoken to Rod on my behalf, supporting me for this position.

Rod was a macho man with slick, light brown hair and a slim physique. An Alabaman with a southern drawl, he was intelligent…and cold. He never interrupted me while I spoke. He just sat back in his chair and listened intently as my confidence grew. Suddenly he leaned forward in his chair, looking at me with dark brown eyes. "When is this corporation's obligation to you going to end?" he asked.

Instantly my heart began to pound through my beautiful suit. I could hear the beats, and I imagined my silk shirt must be moving with each thud of my heart. *Was he kidding with me or what? Where did this come from? Is he angry with me? What kind of question is this?* I flashed back to the convenience store and saw the police officer who made fun of the fact my attacker broke my glasses. I just looked at him. I had not prepared myself for such a question.

"Well?" He said, waiting for an answer.

I just sat there, paralyzed. I didn't know what to say. I had no defense for this; there was no answer. I lost whatever self-confidence I had when I entered. He kept staring at me. I could feel a panic attack coming on as flashbacks filled my mind. I ran out of his office.

Walter and several of the field reps who were my friends were standing outside the door waiting to ask me how it went. I just looked at them, tears flowing down my face as I ran out of the building. I was so embarrassed. I had come all this way. I had worked so hard to be where I was and now this.

What is it about me that brings this out in people? Even my own mother. What am I doing to piss these people off? Why are these people doing this to me?

I went home and cried for hours. I tried to make sense of what had taken place, but found no answers. Roxann came home eager to find out how it went and knew instantly something bad had happened. For the first time, she was speechless. She didn't know what to say to me to make me feel better, nor did I expect her to. I needed a solution. I knew I didn't want to throw all my hard work out the window. I didn't want this little man to ruin the life I had worked so hard to build back up. I needed good advice from someone who was educated and knowledgeable about human behavior and business.

After careful brainstorming Roxann and I decided a letter of complaint to the corporate office in Dallas, Texas, was the only recourse I had. The owners of this company should be aware of the way I had been treated by Rod Cameron. All I had done was interview for a position. I didn't ask for millions of dollars or for a job I didn't think I deserved. I had every right to interview for that position. I wrote the letter and without hesitation, I mailed it.

Thanks to Roxann I was able to get my thoughts together enough to return to work. I wouldn't be able to avoid Cameron, since his office shared space with the district office from which I worked. Walter was in his office when I arrived, and he asked to speak to me. I went in and sat down, holding my feelings tightly, telling myself I would not cry.

"Donna, I know what happened yesterday," Walter said. "For some reason Rod has a bad taste in his mouth about you. Do you know why?" he asked, his voice sounding compassionate.

"No! Yesterday was the first day I ever really talked to him," I replied.

"Well, I'll try talking to him again," he said.

"No. Don't waste your time. Thanks for all you have already done," I said, standing. "I appreciate all you have done for me," I added as I left his office.

A week or so had passed when I walked into the district office after working a store. Walter was waiting for me. "Donna, I need to see you right away," he said, in a tone that was not as nice as usual.

"What?" I asked, feeling close enough to him to be that abrupt.

"Come into my office," he said.

I walked in, and Walter closed the door behind me. Rod was sitting in the office with his back toward me. Walter went around his desk and sat down.

Suddenly Rod turned around in his chair, holding up a piece of paper. "Do you know what this is?" he screamed.

Oh, my God. I am in deep trouble. It must be the letter I wrote. I'll run out...No! I will stand my ground. If he lays one hand on me, I'll kill him. Because if he hits me he'd better kill me. Donna, stop it. He's not going to hit you. Why would he?

"What's going on?" I questioned, willing my voice to stay level.

"What's going on? What's going on?" Rod screamed, slapping the piece of paper with the back of his other hand. He slapped it over and over again. Every time he slapped the paper my body jolted. I looked at Walter, but he wasn't saying anything. I was scared out of my mind. "Do you know what this letter is?" Rod screamed.

"No, sir," I whispered. I raised my eyebrows.

"I'll tell you what it is! A letter from the corporate office in Dallas. Who is the Good Samaritan that helped you do this? I know you couldn't do it on your own," he declared, wadding up the paper and throwing it into the trash.

"I wrote the letter, sir," I said, edging closer to the door.

Rod just stared at me with those dark brown eyes. Walter had his arms crossed, saying nothing, leaning back in his chair.

I didn't want any trouble. I just interviewed for a position. How could things get so out of control? What should I do? Should I quit right here and now? That's probably what he wants me to do. I'm not going to do it! I'm going to stand my ground.

"Will that be all, sir?" I asked.

"Yeah, go!" Rod ordered, waving his hand toward the door in disgust.

I wasn't fired! Something good happened in there. I stood my ground and didn't cry. I felt threatened and didn't react. I held my own and felt good about it. I went up against Rod Cameron, the zone bully. My letter must have made sense to someone if it was answered. Someone was definitely looking out for me, but I would never know who.

Things were never the same between Walter and me again, I think because Rod blamed him. This wouldn't look good on Walter's résumé, since his goal was to become zone manager. He became distant, talking to me only about work-related business. I didn't get the promotion I wanted this time, but after a year it became available and again, I went after it. This time I got it without any problems. Rod and I were forced to work together, and he became my immediate boss. I never backed down, not for one second. I worked hard and didn't make any mistakes.

The new position opened up new opportunities for me. District managers from other zones were calling me to ask what they could do to improve their audit departments. My name was becoming more popular among higher management individuals. My new position involved public speaking, managing more than a hundred stores, interacting with field representatives on a daily basis, attending business meetings in Ocean City, Maryland; Atlantic City, New Jersey; and Las Vegas, Nevada. I was earning $28,000.00 a year with bonus and expenses. I bought myself a new car and paid off all my bills.

I continued my climb to success. I often thought of Ina and how proud she would be of me, knowing I had gone so far in my career. Who would have thought I could come so far?

In 1982 my father died on Valentine's Day. All that drinking finally took a toll on him, and his heart gave out. It's sad, but I can only remember one positive memory I had with my father. A few months before his passing I was in the hospital with yet another bowel obstruction. He came to visit me a few days after my surgery. I couldn't believe it. He looked worn and tired, although he was only 49 years old. He hadn't been drinking that day, either. My father was always a thin man, but this day he looked bloated, sickly. He told me he had driven himself there to see me, and I was flattered. I never saw my father in this state before, and I didn't know how to react. I had an NG tube down my throat and, as usual, I couldn't speak that well.

He sat down and pulled a little stuffed animal out of his pocket, then he began to cry. He handed me the stuffed animal, a little bear just big enough to fit in my hand. I wondered why my father would be crying? *Could it be he is feeling something for me? Is he trying to make peace with God? What?* I was confused. His tears were real, I knew that. I wanted to comfort him, but he had become such a stranger in my life I had no more to offer him. He stayed only a few minutes and left after kissing me on the forehead. I will never forget that day. His memory will live in my heart.

The death of my father brought my family closer together. My mother never apologized for what she had put me through, and she refused to talk about it. I forgave her even though I would never forget that terrible day. Ever since I was a little kid I vowed to always take care of my mother. She had it hard, living with my father, and I had promised myself I would always be there for her, even though if you were to ask her she would say, "I don't need anyone's help." I wish I could say I loved my mother like a daughter should love her mother, but I can't. She hurt me more deeply than anyone could have hurt me during a time in my life when I was so vulnerable. She's a tough lady with a big heart most of the time, but she is human. The fate of our relationship revolved heavily around the months that followed my attack.

After another year I was promoted to field representative in the same zone area, under Reid Lohr, a district manager who went by the name Bud. My responsibilities changed. This position put me right back in the stores. Although I was given a big fat raise, it opened old wounds that became very painful for me. As a field representative my job was to oversee the overall operation of 10 convenience stores by regulating each store's profits and losses and by budgeting and maintaining the integrity of their appearance. It was my responsibility to go to each store daily to collect paperwork, update the owners on promotions and help with any training questions. I would be responsible for buying or repairing equipment, resetting merchandise to current specifications, putting up promotional signage and displays and acting as a security advisor.

In 1985 a new policy was put into place, a policy that would put me in my stores after dark. It was called "Momentum," a buzz word used to boost customer service in the stores. This new policy entailed having field reps surf their stores every shift to make sure the employees were saying hello and thank you to all customers. If observed giving good customer service, the employee would receive a certificate. The franchisees lined their counters with them. The store that was given the most certificates would be given a grand prize.

My stores were doing extremely well, but I was still required to go out every night and give certificates. As time went on, my "Momentum" began to suffer. Being out at night was bad enough for me. I was developing major flashbacks and anxiety as time went on. I tried to buddy up with other field reps, but because our stores were so far apart, it became too time-consuming. I had to make a decision. I couldn't go on like this. I knew this was an important function of my position, but my mind was going haywire with memories from my past. I didn't want anyone to know. I wanted to be like everyone else. The less they knew the better.

I had a few friends outside the company I asked to go with me, but after a while it became too boring and time-consuming for them. Roxann helped as much as she could. She was such a trooper. From the time she met me she was so willing to do whatever it took to help me succeed. I was lucky to have found her. Unfortunately, neither she nor anyone else would be able to help me decide to stay or leave this company. I was changing, and I knew I was in trouble. My fears had returned; anger followed. I couldn't help it. I honestly couldn't help it! I was snapping at people who were nice to me. I knew how hard I had worked to get where I was, and it was disappointing to think I would have to leave. I just couldn't take it anymore. I tried praying, meditating, talking, screaming, crying…but nothing helped me to overcome these feelings.

As fate would have it, Roxann matched a residency program in New Jersey and asked me to come along. Again, I could see the light at the end of my tunnel. My goals would change once more. I accepted Roxann's offer and resigned from the company. I know one person who was thrilled: Rod Cameron. Everyone else with whom I had worked was shocked and upset. I couldn't believe the attention I was given once word got out. Even Bud tried to get me to stay by offering me a position in the real estate department. It was tempting, but I knew it was time for me to move on. I was given all the vacation time I had coming, plus they agreed to let me collect unemployment benefits until I found another job. Walter gave me a wonderful letter of reference, which I took with me. After seven years with this company, I was pleased to say goodbye. I would always remember the many people who helped me.

Roxann and I moved to Bucks County, Pennsylvania, renting a single-family ranch home that needed a lot of work. We spruced it up nicely. Roxann was excellent with her hands and could fix about anything. After a time the house was so warm and comfortable that family and friends never wanted to leave when they came to visit.

Roxann did her residency honorably. Her schedule was grueling, requiring she work 36 hours straight, then home for 12, which she mostly used to sleep. Then she was back at it. This lasted a good two years until she started her psychiatric training at Trenton Psychiatric Hospital. I owed it to her to take care of her during this time, and I was pleased to be able to stay home. I got one dog and then another to keep me company. What good company they were, and good watchdogs, also. I was home alone a lot, and they were great to be around.

I landed a few part-time jobs. They weren't much to talk about, but it was something. I got a computer and began working on my book, a book that would take me years to finish. One day I woke up and decided I wanted to go back to school. I wanted to sell real estate. Without hesitation or needing anyone's approval, I went through the steps to do it. I took a real estate course offered by the Bucks County University. It was great to get my feet wet again and start making something of myself.

After putting in a few semesters and receiving my passing grade, I visited a few broker offices and decided on Century 21 in Yardley, Pennsylvania. Yardley is a beautiful area of historic homes. I was attracted mostly by the old-fashioned feeling it presented—a small town situated along a main street lined with stores and small businesses, canopies and flowers. Nothing I had ever seen compared to its beauty, only blocks away from the Delaware River where many went to have lunch. It was pleasing to the eye and to the heart. This was where I wanted to work. I spoke with the broker, Mary Gracia, an Italian woman who was very professional, yet sweet, with a contagious laugh. She was anxious to have me as soon as I passed my test and became licensed. She invited me to come by any time I wanted to sit with other agents and learn what I could. Most of her agents had been with her for years, and I liked that. Everyone seemed happy to work there.

I got my license after a few tries and started my new career. As luck would have it my first house sold at a quarter of a million dollars. It was a nice paycheck for me and my broker. I'm not saying it was all that easy. It took months of driving people around to finally get that one serious buyer.

First I had to learn the area. Bucks County borders the Delaware River, across from New Jersey and the northern outskirts of Philadelphia. I bought a map book and began my journey. I purchased a new Subaru wagon with money I had saved, giving me security for long travel. I was surprised when I first started taking people out to learn that clients really believed it was okay to make U-turns. It took a lot of hard work, but eventually I caught on. I was determined to do well at this, and so I did.

After my first year I became known to my peers up and down Main Street. I enjoyed walking down to the sidewalk café to make a coffee run for my office and greeting others by name. I felt a part of this little community and safe, as well.

Into my second year I became a little more bold, flexing my wings. I began to take fewer precautions. Driving individuals around, sitting open houses in vacant homes and meeting people at night. Then slowly I could feel my vulnerabilities seeping back in. The memories of my attack were returning, especially after reading that a real estate agent was raped while showing a vacant home in Bristol, a neighboring town. This sort of thing could happen here, as well, and the thought chilled me. The word on the street was that she was only raped, not killed. Little did others know that "only raped" meant being killed inside. I knew exactly what that real estate agent was feeling, and in a subtle way I expressed my opinion when the subject was brought up in my office.

I began to buddy up with a friend, Maryellen, who was a divorced mother of two boys. She and I would share listings and sales, go to closings together and share the profits. This took some money out of my pocket, but it was worth it to me. We had two vacant home listings. Every Sunday she would sit in one while I sat in the other. If someone suspicious came in, I would hop on the phone to Roxann and bend her ear for a while. This didn't seem to bother the potential buyer, and it helped me tremendously.

Maryellen never had an incident happen to her, but I had my first. I was sitting an open house when a man walked in.

He was mid-forties, scroungy looking, wearing a thick jacket. It was spring and the jacket looked out of place. That was my first clue something wasn't right. As he walked in I asked him where he parked, because I knew exactly where all the cars were when I came in. Even though there were several spots available in front of the house, he said he had parked down the street. I immediately became frightened. Something was not right, and my red flag went up, waving frantically. I walked him to the kitchen area where all my papers were and where the back door was, which I quickly opened. He didn't seem particularly interested in the house. Against all my training and sales ethics I allowed him to walk the house by himself. I knew the liability was high, since the house was still furnished. He walked the house, yelling questions to me from the second floor. I was not going to put myself into any situation from which I couldn't escape, so I answered him from below. He then went down to the basement. I told him to go ahead alone and I would be in the kitchen doing some paperwork. While he was down there, he again started yelling questions to me. Then he asked me to come down and show him something. I knew deep in my heart if I did I would be a victim once more, and I refused.

He came up the stairs, not so pleased with me, and cornered me in the kitchen. I kept my hand on the screen door ready to make my escape if necessary. Fortunately, he left. I never was able to get any personal information from him. I felt lucky nothing happened, yet a torrent of emotions flooded my mind, putting my tenure in this field in doubt. I had worked so hard and come so far, but I was not ready to put myself in any bad situation again.

I continued with my job for another six months with mixed emotions. I refused to drive anyone in my car again. They would either follow me there or meet me there. If I sat an open house, I had either Roxann or Maryellen with me.

I had been working with one man for about a year. He lived in the upper-class section of Philly and wanted to move from the everyday hassles of the city to a nice, quiet area in Bucks County. Telling me he was married with two kids, he said he was specifically interested in an old colonial-style home with a barn and 5 acres. I had met with him on several occasions and showed him many properties. One day, hot off the multiple listing computer, came exactly what he was looking for. I called him right away, and he was as excited as I was. I met him at the property, which was vacant. The house was an old colonial with all-wood floors and fireplaces in every room. It was historic, just what he wanted. I thought for sure he would pounce right on it. It had the barn and acreage; everything was perfect. I stayed outside, and while he made his run through the house I admired the beautiful atmosphere. He seemed very pleased when he came out and said he wanted to talk to his wife first before making any commitment to me. I agreed.

A week or so passed, and he called wanting to look at the house again. He said he had some specific questions to ask me, so before I went to the property I called the listing agent and got all the information one could want to know. The house had a radon problem. Because this was so common in the area, it could be treated quite easily. I learned the owners were motivated to sell and would probably negotiate a good price. I was pleased with this information and left to meet him. He was always on time, always wearing a suit and tie, very cordial and professional. I was so excited I was going to sell this home I let down my defenses and made the walkthrough with him in the house.

It was a huge, 5,000-square-foot house with five bedrooms, four baths, formal this and that, yet it was very cozy. I was really surprised it was still on the market after the first week. We walked up to the second floor and I was showing him the master bedroom when all of a sudden he stopped looking around and began coming closer to me. I wasn't sure what that was all about, but I continued my selling. I then brought him into the master bathroom. I went in first, which was a mistake. He blocked the door. I could feel my heart pounding, knowing now something wasn't right. There were no phones there and no people for miles. All I had was my quick sense of danger when my fight or flight emotion kicked in. He was a big, muscular man, and I knew I didn't have a prayer against him. He had never scared me before this moment. I remembered the night of my attack when I was sitting in the car waiting to jolt the ignition of the Nova and looked at my attacker, sensing that he was not paying attention to the car. I felt that same adrenalin rush, knowing I had to get out of there. This man had that same look in his eyes as I walked toward the door to get out. He at first turned to allow me to do this, then put his hands on my shoulders and asked me what my hurry was. I remembered a technique a police officer showed me while I was at the convenience store: when someone has his hands around your neck, you can break the hold by taking your arms up through his and pushing them away. This is exactly what I did, running out of the house and leaving him there. I never looked back to see if he ran after me. I got in my car and left.

I was in sheer panic driving back to the office. I told my broker what had happened and put in my notice of resignation. I then called the listing agent, told him what happened and asked that he go back to the house and lock it up. I did what I needed to do, then went home, where I stayed for weeks without going out. I never returned to the office, giving up all my listings and commissions to Maryellen.

Over the next year or so I did some part-time work, mostly merchandising jobs. I enjoyed it because I was my own boss and was able to work my own hours. Working for American

Greetings was a fun and exciting job. I've always been a card person. After about eight months with them I started developing complications with my health. Because the job entailed so much lifting, I developed a small bowel obstruction caused by adhesions. Back to the hospital I went for another surgery. I made the trip to Maryland and saw my same doctor.

I was becoming very irritable with everything and short with people. I was so tired of starting something, then being forced to quit because of my health and post-traumatic stress. I wasn't sure I would ever amount to anything in my life. *I don't blame employers, I don't blame society, I don't blame God. I blame Kenneth Morgan. He put me here.* I didn't feel I would ever be capable of achieving anything again. My savings were becoming depleted, and I was getting very worried.

In April 1989 Morgan had an administration hearing to determine when he would be eligible for a parole hearing. Subsequently he was scheduled for an August 1991 parole hearing. When I left Maryland, I had written a letter to the Parole Board letting them know my new address; I was glad they notified me. Since I wasn't working, I was able to put all my time into stopping his release. I knew I had to act quickly. I called and wrote to the Parole Board, the Governor, Senator Barbara Mikulski, Assistant State Attorney Frank Weathersbee and Maureen Gillmer, Director of the Witness Protection Agency. I got my family to write letters as well. Even Roxann and my other friends got involved. My sisters got more than 500 names on a petition against his release. I started receiving mail from everyone I had contacted. They copied me on the letters they sent to the parole board and went as far as copying their letters to others who could have some impact.

His first parole hearing was a success for me. He didn't get released.

Later that year Roxann finished her residency, a proud day for her and her family. To me it was another stepping-stone in my life. She decided to start her practice in Florida, and she wanted me to come with her and run her office. I had no experience in the field of medicine, but I did have the management skills. I really felt I had no alternative to her generous offer. I wasn't going to stay in Pennsylvania alone, nor would I ever go back to Maryland. So I agreed.

Florida is a beautiful state. The minute I drove out of Georgia and into the Sunshine State the sky seemed more brilliantly blue and the leaves closer to emerald than mere green. It was clean, and the roads glistened like a welcome mat.

After settling in Roxann's new home I began to feel this was my destiny. I'm not sure how my life could have turned around so quickly, but it did. Roxann's home had three bed-rooms, two bathrooms, a large great room, den and fireplace. There was a big, manmade lake right behind it, giving us beautiful sunsets. It was my dream come true. As a kid I had always wanted to live near the water; the Gulf of Mexico was only 10 minutes away. The neighborhood was quiet and safe. The only noise was from my two dogs, who barked at chameleons and anything else that moved.

While Roxann was busy getting her license and permits, I was out talking to office managers who ran psychiatric of-fices to learn everything I could. Because Roxann was the first female psychiatrist for adults in this area, she did not present a threat to her peers. I worked through myriad forms of insurance companies in my quest to have Roxann become a provider. Medicare, Medicaid, Workers Compensation, Aetna and Principle were many of the companies I solicited. Guidelines, rules, procedure codes, scheduling, billing soft-ware, computer hardware, color coded files, fax machine, phone system, furniture and office supplies were the many items for which I was responsible. I was so busy I didn't have time to think about myself.

We opened the practice successfully. I sat the front desk, greeting patients and doing regular secretarial work; Roxann did the very thing she had worked so long to do. We were a good team. We had good communication, we trusted one another and we worked very hard to make her office the best it could be. My life started to come together just as I had always thought it would.

In late 1992 I purchased my first condo, a medium-sized, first floor, cozy home with two bedrooms and two baths. Things seemed to be going well in all areas, except for my health. Adhesions from so much prior surgery had developed into and around my uterus, causing continuous bleeding and pain. I needed a hysterectomy and lysis of adhesions, a surgery that took two surgeons four hours to complete.

Fortunately I had a full-time secretary, and I ran the practice by remote control while I recovered. Recovery from this surgery was more difficult than any in the past. I realized the older I got, the harder it was to bounce back, and I knew that I needed to be fit and strong so I could keep going forward.

After the surgery I began to live my life. I began to live! I joined a tennis club and started meeting people who enjoyed staying fit and playing tennis. I was surprised at how well I adjusted. My life couldn't have been better. Roxann was paying me a good salary, and I worked to be in the best health I'd ever enjoyed. I could feel myself getting stronger and more confident. I started trusting people again, and they accepted me. The only thing they wanted from me was to be a friend. Even though the prior 15 years of my life had been absorbed with my trauma, I didn't speak of it to my newfound friends. I didn't want anything to change the way they felt about me as a normal human being. It was my past, and no one needed to know about it. Maybe it was all the Florida sunshine that made me feel better, or maybe it was that I finally felt settled. I knew for sure, though, that I was beginning to feel as I thought everyone else felt.

I had spent 15 years wondering what others seemed to know that I didn't. Now I realized that in order to move forward, I had to undo those self-imposed limitations. I didn't have to live in control. I gave it up and just lived. I gave up my limitations and really moved ahead. I knew for certain that I didn't want to go back. At age 38, I had finally reached my destination.

Moving to Florida gave me the opportunity to create myself as I had always wanted to be. I could be seen as healthy, strong, confident and successful. No one knew to think of me as vulnerable, wounded, angry and afraid, as I once was. I liked the person I could be here. I acted friendly, trustworthy and confident. I was, therefore, treated well, trusted and confided in.

In the spring of 1996 I received a notice from the parole board. Morgan's five-year parole hearing was coming up in August. But something was different this time. I didn't have the usual overwhelming sense of fear. I knew I would fight this as I had fought it in the past. At first I was irritated because I would have to divert my attention away from my new life and refocus on Kenneth Morgan again.

As I began reading the notice, I realized the wording of it was different from that of past announcements. It stated in bold letters that the laws in Maryland had changed and victims could now attend the inmate's hearing. In the past, victims were only allowed to write an impact statement, then wait for the outcome by mail. I wasn't sure I had read the information correctly. Extremely anxious, with notice in hand, I made calls to the many people who had helped me in the past. Because the law was so new, most with whom I spoke weren't aware of exactly how the new procedure worked. I was finally told to call Roberta Roper.

Roberta Roper was the mother of Stephanie Roper, who in April 1982 was kidnaped, brutally raped, tortured and murdered. Roberta formed the Stephanie Roper Committee as a result of the public outcry when her daughter's two murderers received sentences that would permit them parole eligibility in less than 12 years. From the family, friends and neighbors who attended the trials in the fall of 1982, the Committee grew to become an effective voice for victims and citizens. The Committee has achieved success in the Maryland General Assembly by proposing and obtaining passage of bills involving sentencing, parole and victims' rights.

I was nervous about making the call because I remembered the headlines of her daughter's capture and murder. Of all people, I who had been through a commensurate trauma, was afraid I wouldn't know what to say. So I sat down with a piece of paper and wrote out my fears and insecurities and literally brainstormed what exactly I was going to say. I remembered how people had said things to me that didn't come out right and were hurtful, and I wasn't about to fall into that with Ms. Roper. I lived through my experience while her daughter had not; I didn't want to come off the wrong way. I needed information from her; I would stick to that.

I picked up the phone and dialed her number. "This is Donna Ferres," I said. "I'd like to speak to Ms. Roper."

"Hold the line," a pleasant female voice said.

My heart was racing. This very important woman was going to talk to me on the phone.

"Hello. Can I help you?"

I couldn't answer instantly. I paused for a moment, looking down at my little sheet of paper, my guide. "Yes...is this Ms. Roper...Roberta Roper?" I asked nervously.

"Yes, it is."

"My name is Donna Ferres. I was given your name by Maureen Gillmer from the Witness Information Department in Annapolis." My voice was shaky.

"Yes, Donna, how can I help you today?" She was very patient.

"I'm a little nervous. Please excuse me," I said.

"Donna, don't be nervous. It seems as though I have heard your name before. Have we ever spoken?"

"No, we haven't, but you may have been aware that back in 1979 I was a victim of a terrible crime," I answered without the help of my piece of paper. I began to relax.

"Yes, Donna, I have heard your name before."

"The reason I'm calling you today is I just received a notice from Paul Davis stating I can attend my offender's parole hearing," I explained, "and was wondering if you knew anything about what will take place."

I could almost feel the wheels in her head turning, and I heard her shuffling papers around. "Yes, I sure can help you," she said. "We finally got the Maryland government to listen to us. Give me your address and I will send you all the information. It is self-explanatory, but basically the new law allows you to attend and watch the procedure. Do you have any specific questions?"

"Not right now," I replied. "I'll wait for the information and call you if I do. Thank you so much for your time. I know you are a busy person....If it's okay, I would like to say I was saddened to hear about your daughter. I'm very sorry."

"Thank you," she said. "She was a beautiful person."

"Please call me with any questions," she added. "Goodbye."

I received the information the following day.

12 Open Parole Hearing

Tucked within the Appalachian-Allegheny Mountains of Western Maryland, in the small town of Hagerstown, sits the Maryland State Correctional Institution for violent criminals. Seventeen years to the month of the attack, my day had finally arrived to stand face-to-face with my attacker. I felt thankful to so many who made this day possible, allowing victims to participate in the parole process.

The August morning was picture perfect. I walked out the side door of our hotel room to the parking lot. The sun's illuminating rays shone from a bright blue sky; the land was beautiful, glistening in a light, misty dew. I stood, invigorated by the cool, brisk air that seemed to coat my body. I was wearing my usual one-piece nylon spandex, covered with shorts and a tee shirt. Because of my increased weight of about 40 pounds over the years, I felt much more comfortable knowing the spandex covered the many scars that lined my torso.

Before starting my morning run, I did my usual warm-up drills, stretching my calf and thigh muscles, rolling my ankles and touching my toes. I ran in place for a minute or so to warm up. Running gave me such pleasure. As a kid and into

adulthood, I had enjoyed all sports—baseball, softball, basketball, walking, biking, horseshoes, dancing and swimming.
It was a very big part of my life that suddenly had been taken
from me. My athletic life had come to a dramatic stop. For
many years I was a couch potato; outside of work I would
stay inside watching television, reading and writing. These
things were important to me, but not when the weather was
so beautiful outside. Post-traumatic stress handicapped my
physical and emotional well-being with flashbacks, fear, panic
attacks, loneliness, pain and lack of trust. In late 1995—thanks
to therapy and being surgery-free for more than five years—
I was able, slowly, to rehabilitate myself back to my love of
sports and athleticism.

My mind raced with intermittent thoughts of the parole
hearing, my family's reaction to learning about it for the first
time and the incident itself as I began my run. Trying to stay
focused on the positive aspect of my purpose here in
Hagerstown, I kept my mind and eyes to the road in front of
me as I began to run harder and faster. Intermittently smiling
between hard breaths, I thought about the ride here with
Roxann, who had generously taken time from her practice to
be with me. She had made the travel plans and hotel arrangements, working with my sisters to make everything go as
smoothly as possible. I thought of the two-hour ride from
my mom's house in Glen Burnie to Hagerstown. How exceptionally pleasurable it was, sharing small talk and laughing
at the continual jokes Roxann was so great at telling, even if
I had heard them all before. My mother sat in the backseat,
comically bantering with me and Roxann, even though her
body language showed anxiety and tension. This was the same
woman who got carsick from riding in the backseat of a car.
Not this time, not for two and a half hours did she mention
any discomfort, so I knew something was occupying her mind.
Tomorrow would be the first time any of my family, with the

exception of my sister Debbie, would see what my assailant looked like.

As I began my run I had goose bumps in the cool air. I was used to Florida weather, and this August morning in Maryland was cold to me. I hadn't thought to bring a jacket. I surveyed the area, wanting to stay within the residential zone. As I proceeded up the road I began to slow my momentum, visualizing and examining the area's perimeters. From my point of view I could see only one residential street that headed straight up a hill. I thought this development must have other roads that ran perpendicular to this one because I could see other homes behind those that lined this road. Assuming the other roads were well behind the small hill that blocked my view, I proceeded uphill. My body temperature warmed quickly as I ran up the lengthy hill, putting my need for a jacket to rest.

Five minutes into my run and finally atop the steep hill, the road suddenly ended at a line of oak trees obscuring a huge cornfield beyond. I couldn't believe there were no other roads! I was a bit upset because I had so much more energy and nowhere to go. I had stopped my run, breaking my momentum, when in my peripheral vision I saw people. I jerked my head in that direction to look closer; I could see a small group of construction men. They were digging holes under one of the massive oak trees. We were only about 20 yards from each other. By the time I focused on them, they clearly had their sights on me. They had all stopped working. It was very unusual! They had this look on their faces as if they have never seen anyone jog before, and I must have looked to them like someone who had never seen anyone dig a hole. The longer we stared at each other the more nervous I became, remembering my attacker was a construction worker.

I could feel panic setting in. My body became hot; sweat ran down my face and neck and my heart was racing when suddenly my mind interposed the face of my attacker onto the faces of the men in front of me. With a blink of my eye I flashed back to the night I first saw my attacker enter my store. This was quickly followed by a fast forward, play-by-play video of my abduction. The smell of body odor and car oil filled my nostrils. It was all so real. And all this time, I stood, frozen, as I had that night, not able to think quickly due to the fear that was overtaking me. My mind was jumping back and forth from then to now, from then to now, from then to now until suddenly, in the distance behind me, I heard a screen door slam. I jumped, startled, but the sound snapped me back into reality. Without hesitation I turned and ran as fast as I could toward the sound. I saw a middle-aged, blue-jeaned man walking to his car. It must have been he who had slammed the door. I yelled, "Thank you," as I ran by. He gave me a puzzled look in acknowledgment.

I was moving like a marathon runner to the finish line, leaving behind the demons that have haunted me for years, when I finally reached the hotel. Breathless, I sat on the hood of our rental car to calm myself. Sweat beads dripped from my forehead onto my glasses and off my chin. I could hear my heart pumping vigorously. Angry at my vulnerability, I slowly walked back to the room, wiping away tears and putting on a fake smile to avoid upsetting my mother. I gave a quick greeting and went into the bathroom, which was conveniently located just inside the front door. I locked the bathroom door behind me, pulled off my clothes and jumped into the shower to dispose of the fermenting stench of my attacker, which I remembered so vividly encasing me. I stood, it seemed like an eternity, under the hot shower, whimpering powerlessly against my mind's ability to recall every sensory detail.

Slowly I began to calm myself with positive thoughts and rationalization. As I stood under the beating, warm water that massaged the back of my neck, a loud noise that seemed to shake the wall startled me. I quickly shut off the water and could hear faint voices, and I assumed my sisters had arrived. I wiped the steam off the mirror and practiced facial expressions that would make me appear happy; but the pain in my eyes showed a different picture.

Carting their own internal pain and anguish, Debbie and Barbara arrived together. As I came out of the bathroom, they immediately embraced me with warm affection. Although they had left Baltimore at 4:00 A.M., they were energetic and boisterous. We all talked at the same time about everything except why we were gathered here. Feeling somewhat obtuse, I could only watch as the suitcases were carried out of the room by my family. Roxann noticed my obvious lethargy, took my arm and led me out of the room to the others who were waiting in the hallway. From that moment on, each of us became a link, all connected, forming a solid chain of tenacious courage.

We stopped in the hotel's restaurant for a cup of coffee and toast to ease our rumbling stomachs. As we were seated I knew they were looking at me to set the tone. If I talked about *it*, they knew it was okay to talk about. We ordered coffee. I pulled from my fanny pack five small round pins that read simply, "Victim Rights." I had them made up especially for us. I held them in my hand and clicked my water glass with my spoon. All eyes fell upon me.

I said. "Here we are, all dressed up and looking fine. This pin I hold in my hand will represent this day as our day, the day we unite to do the right thing, not only for me but for all victims. Today is much more important than anyone could imagine. Today I am surrounded by the most important people in my life, who have supported me and helped me to survive the worst thing that has ever happened to me. Today, we all face the person who took so much from our lives. I want to thank you all very much."

Each took her coffee cup and clanged it together with the others, in unison. I passed out the pins and we proudly put them over our hearts. No tears were shed, no other words were spoken. That feeling, that moment, will be with me forever.

Roxann broke the tension by telling my sisters the story of our experience the night before. Her comical way of talking, facial expressions and hand gestures kept the attention of her listeners. She began by telling how we had gone to visit the prison grounds beforehand so that we wouldn't get lost today. The sign read, "Maryland Correctional Institution," so we had followed the narrow, paved road that stopped at the prison. She got out of the car at the gate and was approached by a stone-faced guard. She told the guard that we would be back in the morning for a parole hearing and asked him what we would need to do. Maintaining a stern posture, the guard only stared at her. Quick on her toes, she told him that in the car was the victim who came from Florida to address the parole commissioners. Suddenly, without hesitation, the guard's demeanor changed completely. A broad smile came over his face, and his eyes sparkled as he registered what she told him. They shook hands and introduced themselves. Without asking for any other information, he gladly gave her the instructions we needed. She got back into the car and rolled down her window. The guard, smiling and waving, wished us luck, and we heard him yell up to the guards in the tower, telling them who we were. Feeling calmer and reassured, we left to find the hotel, chatting about our enlightening experience.

Buoyed by Roxann's account, we left the restaurant, packed ourselves into the car and left for the prison. As I sat between my sisters in the backseat, Roxann made us aware we were about to turn into the prison grounds. Ahead in the distance we could see the 30-foot, razor-wired fencing that enclosed the English-style, Georgian prison building constructed of large stone. A huge antenna loomed atop its gabled roof. Several secondary Georgian clones were attached to the main structure by concrete walkways. Apart from and directly outside the fenced area stood a linear, brick guard tower with a circular glass enclosure at its peak, in which we could see two armed deputies standing.

Anxiously taking the closest parking spot, Roxann offered Xanax all around. Everyone indulged in a small half-tab. We walked toward the visitors building, a one-story brick building with barred windows, then entered through two heavy, red metal doors. Immediately to our right was a raised counter where we were told to sign in by a female uniformed guard. The atmosphere was cold and stark and echoed our every word and footstep. After showing our identification and parole letters, we were instructed to remove our jewelry, surrender our purses and put them into a locker. A police band radio squawked continuously. There was a large waiting area with empty rows of seats. We were the only outsiders. We were eventually confronted by a young male guard who guided us through a metal detector, each of us setting the alarm off, causing the female guard to approach us with a wand. Ironically, our Victim Rights buttons were setting off the alarm.

Escorting us through a rear door, the young deputy waved to the guards in the tower. A loud buzzer sounded and the heavy gate opened. We hurried through together and awaited another buzzer for the second gate. Once on the inside we could clearly see the immaculate, manicured lawns, landscaped with blooming marigolds and impatiens. Its decorative beauty reminded me of the movie *Wizard of Oz* when Dorothy and Toto landed, as we followed the brick pathway to the main entrance. The garden's aroma and beauty, while totally incongruous, were comforting.

A thick skeleton key unlocked the massive metal door that led into the main prison building. The door slammed closed behind us, causing a continuous echo along the stone walls and numerous barred gates that appeared in front of us, stirring a commotion beyond our view, inmates yelling out obscenities. We walked single file, imitating the Keystone cops, making our way through the gated doors into a large, sparse room. To our left were three occupied cells. I kept my eyes forward, fully aware my attacker was among them.

Here I am after 17 years, I thought to myself. *This is my day, my opportunity to face the one person who changed my life, and yet I can't turn my head in his direction.*

My emotions bounced back and forth with every step I took. One second feeling strong and powerful, the next feeling weak and vulnerable. "Stay focused," I murmured. To our right were three large folding tables littered with piles of paper. About 10 people sat facing a glass-enclosed room to our left, just beyond the cells. They were dressed professionally, so I assumed they were observers. They were so engrossed with the paperwork in front of them they didn't acknowledge our presence. The deputy directed us to be seated, pointing to a large area with six metal folding chairs placed haphazardly in close proximity to the hearing room, which I now could see was enclosed on all sides.

Feeling strong and powerful, I took the initiative to arrange the chairs in an organized manner, giving me the best view of the proceedings and of my attacker. Debbie sat on one side of me, Barbara on the other. My mother and Roxann sat directly behind. A 1-foot square box speaker hung above the glass enclosure facing us. Inside the room we could see the parole commissioners, one woman and two men, sitting on one side of a conference table, flipping through copious files.

History was in the making this 19th day of August, 1996. Prior to this new Maryland law that allowed victims to attend parole hearings, only a victim-impact statement would be accepted and had to arrive 30 days before the hearing. No direct communication to the parole commissioners could be made. But I knew if I could get enough letters out to important people, the parole commissioners would invariably know where I stood. That's what I had done the first time. My statement was sent out by certified mail to the parole board, the governor of Maryland, Maryland senators and congresspersons, the district attorney, victims rights advocates and the parole board directors. My mom, sisters, friends, doctors and therapists sent their letters on the same day mine was sent, so the impact was obvious. Anyone who was important in the process knew Kenneth Morgan was coming up for parole. Although this painstaking procedure had taken its toll on my emotions and my life, I had fought for my right to keep Kenneth Morgan behind bars. I was prepared to do it every five years for the rest of my life—or his—if necessary.

We had been seated but a few seconds when we were asked by a deputy to go into the parole room and speak with the parole commissioners. This really floored me because during my many phone calls I had been told that the new law only allowed me to observe. I wouldn't be allowed to speak at all. This was my big opportunity to talk face-to-face with the people who would be making the decision to keep Kenneth Morgan behind bars, and I hadn't prepared anything. My mind went into overdrive. I do well when I have time to prepare, but when I am spontaneously put on the spot, I crumble. *Oh my gosh, what am I going to say?* I needed more time to prepare. I needed a small room where I could sit in silence and put my thoughts in order so I wouldn't sound like a raving maniac to these important people. I began to panic. This invitation didn't seem to bother my family or Roxann as they quickly walked toward the room. Preoccupied with my thoughts and lagging behind, I realized my family had entered the parole room without me.

Suddenly and without warning I looked up and saw…him. There he was, Kenneth Morgan, standing 4 feet before me in the hall with a guard. He had been removed from his cell and was approaching the hearing room when our eyes locked. At first I didn't notice who this person was until I saw behind his well-groomed silver beard, Hawaiian shirt and blue jeans. Then it hit me. *There he is!* This is the same man who came to my store in torn, smelly denim clothes, reeking of alcohol and body stench. I began to tremble as the terror once again overwhelmed me. For an instant I saw him put his sights on me like a hunter on his prey, watching its every move. This time, though, I retreated into the safe arms of my loved ones, who saw my fear and quickly rescued me from the hallway.

Bent over, looking down at the floor, I held my knees to support my trembling limbs. My soft cries could be heard around the room, causing a meltdown of emotion to erupt from my family. Without hesitation, the female parole commissioner approached me, empathetically apologizing for the accidental confrontation. She handed me a tissue. Barbara, who had always protected me as a child, didn't hesitate to express her feelings, by saying, "This is exactly why you need to keep that animal behind bars."

The room became silent, and I could feel everyone's eyes focused on me. I'm not a person who likes to be the center of attention. I stood up and wiped the tears from my face, unequivocally announcing, "I'll be just fine," knowing he had been returned to his cell. I couldn't stop my body from trembling, but I hid it well. Sensing that I had regained my composure, my family wasted no time expressing their feelings to the commissioners.

I felt myself detach, listening to the many conversations that were going on around me in this small 12- by 10-foot, glass-enclosed room. My mind struggled to focus on my purpose. As hard as I tried to rid my mind of him and that terrible night, it was too powerful to overcome so quickly—not seeing him for so many years and then face-to-face.

Mr. Frank Pappas, the lead commissioner, said, "Donna, we will be going through the events of that night in detail. Do you feel up to it?"

When I nodded, he apologized and then explained the procedure.

As we returned to our designated area outside the interviewing room, my once-felt courage to center myself in full view of Morgan, and he of me, dissipated. He had seen me. I knew what it had done to me, and I didn't want him to see me again. I moved my chair out of his view, off to the side away from the plexiglass window. One guard quickly moved toward me, not realizing my intention was only to avoid visual contact with Kenneth Morgan and nothing more. Then he realized it and backed off.

They brought Kenneth Morgan in. He was seated facing the commissioners with the stack of files on the table between them. The men and women monitoring the procedure watched in the distance. I still didn't know who they were or what they were doing there.

Seated, my body trembled uncontrollably as if I had developed Parkinson's Disease. My sister Debbie leaned forward in her chair to get as close to him as possible, focusing a cold, vicious stare directly at him, making me smile a bit. Barbara listened intently as they began to question him. Roxann stretched her arm across to where I had moved and patted my knee, but her eyes never left the proceedings.

I sat quietly listening to the voice of the lead parole officer, Frank Pappas, through the speaker as he read the contents of the file. Every sentence he read clicked another slide into my mind's projector.

I was impressed by the systematic order in which the file was presented, beginning with the sentence Morgan was given, then the homicide investigation report that ultimately implicated him when a search of his bedroom by police found my broken glasses on his dresser. In addition—a plus for the case—the police found a rare coin that belonged to a young woman who had been robbed at gunpoint just weeks prior, further implicating him. I was convinced Morgan would have gone on to become a serial murderer if not caught.

Pappas, flipping pages in the file, introduced the presentence report that included the guilty plea and detailed confession presented to the court in 1980. As his words filtered through the speaker, my body became very warm with guilt. For the very first time my family would hear the real truth of that night. They would hear how I walked outside the convenience store to help him with his car. Would they hear that I had gone out voluntarily and consequently, believe I had brought this on myself? My mind's worry implanted negative thoughts of my family rejecting me, as I had rejected myself over the past 17 years. No sooner were the words read by the parole officer than it passed, without a flinch from any of my family, or it seemed that way.

The time had come for Kenneth Morgan to speak. Safe beyond the plexiglass window, I prepared myself. Commissioner Frank Pappas asked him to explain the events of that night as he remembered them.

"Well…" He stopped. His voice chilled my skin, making the hair on my arms stand up.

Commissioner Pappas spoke again. "What was the victim's name?" he asked.

"Um…um…um, I don't know," Morgan replied. His voice sparked a rapid succession of strobe light flashbacks of the events I so vividly recalled.

"Are you telling this panel you don't know the name of the person whom you brutally attacked and almost murdered?" Pappas asked in a louder tone.

I could hear my sisters' whispers to each other but couldn't turn my head toward them.

"No, I can't even give it a guess. Do you want me to continue?" Kenneth Morgan asked in a soft tone.

"Yes, continue," Pappas said, his feelings of disgust obvious in his voice. "But keep in mind, the panel may have some questions while you're speaking. Also, please speak up."

"Well, that night I had been drinking," Morgan said, "and smoking pot. I was driving around and stopped at a convenience store. The store was busy with people so I left and went to another store right up the road. There were no people there except the girl in the store. I went into the store and bought a drink. I recognized her but didn't know her name. We talked a few minutes and then a couple of ladies came in the store, so I left. I sat in my car watching her mop the floor. I waited and realized there was no customers. I was feeling angry and felt like hurting someone, so I decided to hurt her—"

"Why her?" Pappas asked, interrupting.

"Because of opportunity!" Morgan exclaimed with a shrug.

"What happened next?" Pappas queried.

"I made up a lie to lure her to my car because the store was so brightly lit and could be seen from the road. I put the hood up on my car and went back into the store. She was still mopping when I told her my Nova wouldn't start. She said she had a Nova, too, same year, and had often had that same problem with the ignition. She offered to call an all-night car repair place for me. I told her I only needed her to turn the ignition key while I set the points. She hesitated for a minute, then followed me out and got into my car. Once she was out there, it was easy to grab her. When she tried to run back in the store, I put my knife to her throat and threw her in my car. I took her to a secluded area and raped her, then tied her pants around her neck and dragged her back to my car. Then I brought her to a gravel pit area and stabbed her 'til she died, and left." There was no remorse in his voice.

"What happened next?" Pappas prompted.

"I...um...drove to a friend's house in Baltimore City and told them what I did and turned myself in. The police came and I was arrested."

"Did you think you killed this girl?" Pappas pressed.

"Oh, yeah, definitely, I killed her," he said with a half smile on his face.

"Is there something funny about that?" Pappas yelled.

"No...she wasn't dead, that's all," Morgan replied, looking down at the table, somewhat taken aback by the fury in Pappas's voice.

I could hear the groans and moans from my family, the twitching in their chairs while Kenneth Morgan spoke, reacting to what he was saying.

"When you kidnaped the victim, was your intention to kill her?" Parole Commissioner Patricia Cushwa interjected.

"Yeah," he said. "Uh...I wanted the girl from the other store, but I couldn't get to her."

"Did the victim scream or try to get away?" Cushwa asked, knowing my side of the story from the many impact statements I had written.

"She tried to get away once, but I punched her a few times and she settled down. I don't remember her screaming, though," Morgan stated with a puzzled look on his face.

"Where did you punch her?" Cushwa asked.

"In the face. I knocked her out!"

"Did you force her into oral sex?" Cushwa asked.

"Yes."

"Did you have intercourse with her?" Cushwa queried.

"Yes, several times."

"For how long did this go on?" Cushwa asked.

"I don't really know. It was a long time…hours."

"Did the victim put up a fight?" Cushwa continued.

"No, not really. I had the knife on her the whole time…you know, on her throat. She kept talking to me, trying to persuade me to let her go 'cause she had a baby at home that really needed her. And she said if I let her go she wouldn't tell anyone about what happened. All I wanted was for her to shut up and stop talking to me," Morgan said in an angry tone.

"Did this bother you, that she had a child?" Cushwa questioned.

"No, it didn't bother me."

"Do you regret what you have done to this victim?" It was Cushwa's closing question.

"Yes, I feel bad about what I did, especially knowing the girl was the sister of someone I knew." He looked out toward Debbie.

"You bastard!" Debbie blurted, glaring at him.

"That's all I have," Cushwa said as her facial expression changed to disgust.

"Your file indicates you have continued to do drugs since you have been incarcerated," Pappas said as he flipped through the file. "What kind of drugs do you do?"

"Pot," Morgan replied. "I've done that in here.…Uh…that's all."

"Was this the drug you did on the outside?" Pappas asked.

"I used to sniff glue."

"What other drugs?" Pappas questioned.

"I took everything I could get my hands on," Morgan admitted. "My friends would come over to my house with all kinds of stuff—pills, powder—and I would try it out for them, to make sure it was safe."

"What do you mean, safe?" Pappas asked, puzzled.

Morgan shrugged. "You know, to make sure there was no strychnine or poison in it."

"Do you feel you should be released?" Pappas put it quite bluntly.

"No, I did a bad thing and this is where I should stay."

Pappas wanted the record to be clear on this. "So what you are saying is that you deserve to be incarcerated?"

"Yes," Morgan replied.

"You know that you are entitled to another hearing in five years, but only at your request," Pappas stated. "Otherwise you will continue your life sentence. Do you understand?"

"Yes, I understand," Morgan responded, "if I want it."

"Is there anything you would like to say to the board before we make our determination?" Pappas asked.

"No," was the response.

"Are there any other questions the board may have for this inmate?" Pappas looked around the room, pausing. When no one responded, he said, "Okay, then, we will take a few minutes and call you back in."

The inmate was escorted from the hearing room and back to his holding cell. My mom, wiping her tears with Kleenex, seemed overwhelmed, but she was handling it very well. I knew it was difficult for her and felt bad she had to go through this. I sat silently while Roxann and my sisters spoke softly to each other. After all that, I still anticipated the worst. This son-of-bitch could be released. I don't know why I was even thinking this. His own admission he should stay in jail should have been reason enough for me to know he wouldn't be released. Yet so many emotions were coursing through my body, I didn't know anything from anything. I just wanted to yell out, "Help me!" I don't know why.

I saw Commissioner Pappas motion to the deputy to bring the inmate back. My body was one big muscle cramp. Morgan reentered the hearing room and sat in the same chair. When Pappas began to talk, I suddenly stood up from my chair. It wasn't something I had planned to do; I just did it. My action made the deputies nervous and they quickly walked toward me, but I stood my ground, even though everybody was looking at me. No one knew what my intentions were, nor did I. I placed my hands together in front of me and waited for the board's determination, as though I were a defendant being sentenced.

"It is the recommendation of this board to deny your parole based on the findings of this hearing. In five years you have the right to another hearing, only at your request," Commissioner Pappas stated. "That is all." The inmate was dismissed.

My sisters cheered with relief. I smiled nervously, relieved that, chances were, I wouldn't need to return, since by his own admission he believed he deserved to be here and rejected any future hearings. Now I could safely say I would work hard to put a period to this part of my life.

Relaxed and giddy, we gathered our belongings and left the prison. My mother kissed the palm of her hand and touched it to the ground outside. We all walked to the car with our arms around each other, side by side. The smiles on our faces told a story of solidarity. Once at the car I grabbed my camera and asked a passerby to take our picture in front of the prison. As we were lining up for the camera, a female guard came running toward us. She adamantly explained we couldn't take pictures of the prison. Because this was so important to me my sisters began to protest, but I asked them not to. I didn't want anyone to interfere with this moment. We just smiled and told her okay. The woman holding the camera stayed, and after the guard made her way back inside, we took the picture.

From left to right: Debbie, Donna, Roxann, Mom and Barbara, all smiling triumphantly as they stand in front of the prison directly after the Open Parole Hearing on August 19, 1996.

At age 45, I find that I have become the person I started out to be. I have always believed if I worked hard enough I could get anything I wanted from life.

As I look back now, I see that I have learned many things. I gave Kenneth Morgan a lot of power. I allowed him to stay in my head and dictate my life. I gave up my life for him and what he represents. As silly as that sounds, I did it. Every man was a rapist; anyone could overpower me; no one was safe; no place was safe. I could not defend myself because of what he had done to me. I did not have enough confidence in myself to fight back. What happened to me was terrible, but what was worse was the person I subsequently became. I spent all my time trying to control every situation. I was anxious, guarded, uncomfortable, suspicious and rigid—all in an effort to keep myself safe and invulnerable. I was more a prisoner in the world than he could ever be.

Post-traumatic stress disorder (PTSD) is real. I lived with it for a very long time. My book describes many instances in which reexperiencing symptoms altered my state of mind with:

- frequent, sudden and upsetting memories about the event.
- repeated, distressing dreams.

- flashbacks.
- strong mental and emotional pain when I saw people, places or things that reminded me of the event (even smells could trigger the event).
- physical reactions (such as shakiness, fast heartbeat, perspiring) when I saw people, places or things that reminded me of the event.

I know now that I had avoidance and numbing symptoms:

- I made efforts to avoid thoughts, feelings and conversations that reminded me of the event.
- I tried to avoid activities, places and people that reminded me of the event.
- I stopped enjoying or taking part in activities that I once enjoyed.
- I felt detached from family and friends.
- I believed that certain important life goals would not be fulfilled.

I also had what is called hyper-arousal symptoms. I constantly scanned my environment for danger and was so busily preoccupied with potential harm that:

- I had problems falling asleep and staying asleep.
- I had angry outbursts and was irritable.
- I had problems concentrating.
- I was physically tired all the time, yet overly alert.
- Any noise startled me, causing my body to jump.

Post-traumatic stress disorder is a normal reaction to an abnormal amount of stress. If untreated and coupled with life stresses, it could lead to a chronic depression.

It has been a long road for me, and I hope the reader has gotten something from my book. I am glad to be here to tell my story. I believe there are many like me out there, and I hope my book reaches out to let others know they are not alone in their recovery. Perhaps, too, this book will help those with loved ones suffering through these symptoms. I was blessed to have family who loved me enough to understand this was not going to go away easily; they stood by me. From the get-go, I never stopped pursuing my battle to keep Kenneth Morgan behind bars. I lived that night with the same perseverance that I live each day. That is who I am. I was a survivor, but now I am much more.

In closing I should like to speak to those who know a person who has been a victim of crime. I understand it is hard for those around us to know the right thing to say or the right thing to do. My first step to recovery was explaining to those around me how I felt and what I needed. I can tell you what helped me. I have listed a few things I believe satisfied my needs.

- Show interest in their concerns.
- Give hugs whenever possible. (Always ask if giving someone a hug is okay first, honoring their space.)
- Don't stop calling.
- Support their interests with invitations and don't get angry if they turn you down.
- Accept them as they are.
- Don't judge.
- Don't make light of the event.
- Don't say you understand.
- Deal with your anger yourself. Let the victim be angry.
- Deal with your anger yourself. Let the victim cry.
- Be a friend. Don't expect the victim to console you. This is not about you; understanding this fact is being a friend.

Appendix I: Feeling Safe

I felt it important to add this chapter for a couple of reasons. At the age of 24, I never thought, not once, I would ever be a victim of rape. If I knew then what I know now...

When I was hired to work in the convenience store, I was trained on what to do if I was robbed. I was shown videotapes and booklets and taught about theft. I knew to make a money drop (placing money through a tube into a safe that can only be opened by management) if I saw a suspicious person. I knew to do exactly as I was told if confronted by a robber. This would keep me safe. I felt safe having this information because I knew what to expect, or so I thought.

Because I never even considered personal injury as a possibility, I was ill-prepared to prevent it.

I am convinced the crime of rape depends on two things: *vulnerability and opportunity.*
I am also convinced that as the awareness level of potential victims rises, the crime level will drop.

Who Is the Victim?

Every person, regardless of race, age, gender, socioeconomic status, or lifestyle is a potential victim of a personal attack. Women are the most targeted when they are alone and often by someone they know or recognize.

Sexual Assault

Myths about sexual assault continue to exist without basis.

- **Myth 1: *The victim is always young and attractive.***
  It is sad many believe what they see on television and at the movies. The truth is there are no stereotypical victims.
- **Myth 2: *The person provokes the attack.***
  Rapists select their victims on the basis of opportunity.
- **Myth 3: *The act of rape is perpetrated for sexual gratification.***
  Rapists have consenting relationships, but choose to rape, both because they enjoy overpowering and degrading their victims and to relieve their feelings of hostility, aggression and inferiority.
- **Myth 4: *Sexual assault is provoked by either a woman's mode of dress or her mannerisms.***
  The truth is there are no stereotypical victims.

Fact: The crime of rape bears a close resemblance to violent crimes such as robbery and aggravated assault more than it does to sexual intercourse with a consenting woman. This is something all potential victims, their families and prospective jurors should know. *Vulnerability and opportunity* are the key factors that cause females of all ages to be potential victims.

Who Is the Rapist?

The rapist is a man who is emotionally unstable yet deals with life on a day-to-day basis in a reasonably normal and/or competent manner. He is often an apparently normal individual but one who has difficulty relating to others in a permanent or lasting fashion. According to the reported cases of sexual assault, the assailant is often a friend, date, relative, coworker, or casual acquaintance. Keep in mind that exhibitionists and "peeping toms" should be considered as potentially dangerous since these acts may be only part of a fantasy that includes rape.

Thirty-five sexual predators were interviewed to find out what they look for in a victim. According to the national victims center, 1 in 8 women will be raped.

The following are some of the things rapists look for:

1. **Women alone.** This is the number one thing rapists look for. Most rapes occur between 5 A.M. and 8 A.M. Walk with someone else or in a group especially going and coming from a parking lot.

2. **Loose clothing.** The rapists interviewed said they look for women wearing loose clothing they can easily grab, tear, hang on to and cut off. Overalls were a favorite of most men who carried scissors with them.

3. **A specific area.** Parking lots for grocery stores, gyms, office buildings and malls are the most common place for rapists to prowl because women are tired and have their guards down.

4. **Hair.** Many of the rapists said they targeted women with long hair or with hair in a ponytail, braid or bun because those styles are easy to grab to control the woman.

5. **Public restrooms.** Rapists said they lurk around or in a women's restroom because women's pants are already down and they are in a small space. Many disguised themselves as women.

6. **Daydreaming.** The rapists target women who appeared lost or walked with their eyes downward. Also, those who wore Walkmans, were talking on a cell phone, fumbling with keys or appeared intoxicated were targets.

7. **Awareness of rapist.** Almost all of the rapists said they would not have attacked the woman if they knew she could identify them.

Why Does This Crime Occur?

Sexual assault is a crime, always. Rapists are emotionally unstable and view their victims as objects upon which to vent their hostility, aggression, frustration or insecurity. They do not view their victims as human beings at the moment and sexual gratification is not a motive for their crime. Rapists humiliate and degrade their victims, to make them lesser beings than they are. Too often the fantasy they are acting out carries with it the danger of physical harm in addition to the act of rape itself.

Where Does Sexual Assault Occur?

Most reported incidents occur in the home of the victim or in the home of the assailant. There are other hazardous areas of which you should be aware:

- Remote areas, vacant lots
- Public parks
- On the street
- Alleys
- Deserted buildings
- Stairwells
- Parking lots and garages
- School campuses
- Beaches at night
- School playgrounds
- Shopping centers and malls
- Laundromats

Preventative Measures

- Exterior doors should be of solid wood core construction.
- Use quality deadbolt locks on all exterior doors, including the door from the garage to the house.
- Have the locks on all exterior doors rekeyed when you move into a new house or apartment.

- Install a peephole viewer with a maximum 180-degree angle in the front door.
- Keep your garage door closed at all times.
- Sliding glass doors usually come equipped with inadequate locks. You can secure them with inexpensive key locks, by a hole drilled through the overlapping frames and pinned with a nail and with anti-slide blocks. Screws protruding in the track will prevent the door from being lifted out.
- Sliding glass windows can be secured in the same fashion as the doors.
- Use key locks or pin the frames on all double-hung windows.
- Remove operator handles from awning windows, but keep nearby in case of fire.
- Replace all jalousie doors and windows, if possible. If not, you can secure them by using a heavy gauge mesh or grillwork to make sure they have a quick release feature on the inside for use in case of fire.
- Good lighting is a deterrent to crime. Install adequate exterior lighting at all vulnerable entrances to the house. In an apartment, join with other tenants in demanding good lighting around entrances and in hallways, parking areas, courtyards and laundry and game rooms.

Don't Open the Door to Strangers

- Check the identity of callers through the peephole in the door, and instruct your children to get you if the caller is someone they don't know.
- If someone comes to the door asking to use the phone for an emergency, offer to make the call for them, but don't let them in the house.
- Request identification by all repairmen and maintenance men. Check their credentials by calling the number in the phone book, not the ID on the card. In an apartment, call the apartment manager.

- Be alert to suspicious phone calls. Do not give out personal or family information or information about your neighbors, regardless of who the caller says he represents; instruct your children to do the same.
- Don't advertise that you live alone. When answering the door call out a "fake" name like "I'll get it, Joe." List your last name and first initial only on the mailbox and front door and in the telephone book. Consider adding a "dummy" name or names on your mailbox to give the appearance of having roommates.
- While home at night, keep a light on in more than one room to make it appear that you are not alone. While away from your dwelling at night, make it look and sound occupied. Leave a radio on and turn lights on in more than one room, plus the bathroom.
- Don't hide an extra key outside. Rapists and burglars know all the best spots.
- Keep you doors locked even if leaving for only a moment, such as going to the neighbors', the pool or game room, a store or even while in the backyard. Rapists and burglars are opportunists.
- Don't leave underwear or bathing suits out on the line, balcony or clothes rack at night. This could attract a rapist or "peeping tom."
- Be wary of neighbors or casual acquaintances who make it a habit of "dropping in" when no one else is home.
- Even though it may sound like an obvious point, remember to keep drapes or blinds drawn when changing clothes, undressing or retiring for the night.

In Your Car

- Invest in a cellular phone to have available for emergencies.
- Whenever possible, park in a well-lighted area.
- Always lock your car.

- Have your keys in your hand when leaving home or work.
- If working late, try to have a friend or security guard accompany you to your car.
- Before getting in the car, be sure to check the floor of the backseat.
- When driving, keep your doors locked.
- If you think you're being followed, do not drive home. Drive to the nearest gas, fire or police station or to the nearest well-lighted area where there are people.
- If you have car trouble on a busy road, raise the hood and then wait inside the car with the doors locked and the windows up. If a motorist stops, crack your window slightly and ask them to call the police.
- If you have car trouble in a remote area, use your best judgment; raise the hood and stay in the vehicle if you feel safe, or raise the hood and find a safe secluded area away from the vehicle where you cannot be seen until a police officer arrives.
- If you want to help a disabled vehicle, don't get out of your car. Drive to the nearest well-lighted area with a phone and call the police.
- Don't pick up a hitchhiker or hitchhikers under any circumstances.
- Don't pull over for flashing headlights. If it is an emergency vehicle or the police, there will be flashing red or blue lights on top of the car.

On the Street

- The rapist is looking for a woman who appears vulnerable. So keep alert and walk with purpose and confidence.
- If you are being harassed from someone in a vehicle, turn and walk in the opposite direction.
- Try to head for lights and people.
- Don't stop to give directions to a driver or pedestrian. However, if you feel you must, maintain enough distance

to prevent being grabbed and dragged into the car or an alley.

- If you think you are being followed, don't go home. Go to a safe place where there are people or lights.
- Don't hitchhike or accept rides from a stranger. It is dangerous. Once you get in the car, you have lost control of the situation.
- If you plan to do some walking, wear clothing and footwear that give ease and freedom of movement.

Individual Reactions

No one knows how he or she will react when actually confronted with the threat of sexual assault. In any crisis one must rely on his or her own response based on multiple factors.

Know Yourself

- Every person is a special individual whose attitudes and reactions are the result of a combination of many factors: family, religious convictions, social interactions with others, basic personality traits and physical condition.
- The complexity of sexual assault is that you will never know exactly how you would handle such a situation. This will all depend on what the circumstances are, who you perceive the attacker to be and what your basic personality is.
- Since you can't know what the circumstances might be or who your assailant might be, it is of utmost importance for you to think about who you are and how you would reason with different situations.
- It may be of prime importance to you to come away with the least possible physical injury.
- You may fear the rape more than you fear the physical injury.

- The very thought of being assaulted may make you so angry that you would rather face the risk of serious injury.
- The way you react may depend on your physical condition.

The list of "ways and whys" of your reaction is infinite, and for this reason, it is important you understand the different alternatives of tactics on how you could best cope with a rape situation.

The woman does not provoke the attack. It is the attacker's problem with which you are dealing, and which has become an invasion of your well-being. Attempt to reach him as a human being so that you seem less of an object to him.

It should be understood that the rapist does not understand or recognize the rights of an individual.

Rapists are opportunists. They look for what they perceive to be vulnerable targets. All rapists have the potential to be violent. This would be a most important consideration when determining alternatives to choose in any given situation.

Alternative Tactics to Use If Attacked

- No one can tell you a specific tactic to use, for what works for one woman may not work for you.
- You, as an individual, must deal with a rapist as an individual. You must take into consideration the time and place, for these too, will have a bearing on your reaction. Panic and fear are perfectly normal reactions.
- You should know what alternative tactics are and what their positive and negative factors are so that you will have the knowledge and awareness to handle the situation in a manner that is most likely to avert the sexual assault.

A Diverting Noise

- This is probably a better tactic to use when you have some advance warning of a situation. It is only useful if there is someone nearby to hear the noise and be willing to come to your aid or frighten off the assailant.
- Sometimes screaming "Fire!" or "Call police!" (not rape or help) or blowing a whistle you have readily available may frighten away your assailant and call attention to your situation. But it may antagonize him. Screaming could make him angrier and he may beat you or strangle you to keep you quiet. You must weigh the odds, depending on the situation, if this tactic is to be successful.

Running

- The risk with this tactic is whether he can and will run faster than you and overpower you.
- Unless you are reasonably certain you can get a good lead and reach safety before he overtakes you, this may be a risky tactic.

Gaining a Psychological Advantage

- Panic and fear are perfectly normal responses; however, if you have mentally prepared yourself (in advance) by accepting the fact that you could someday find yourself in a rape situation and have thought about what you might do, it may decrease the trauma and allow you to react more quickly in coming to grips with the problem.
- This is an intermediate tactic when you need that precious time to get over the initial panic or fear. Quickly survey your situation so you can begin to defuse your assailant's anger.
- This tactic can take many forms: going limp, sinking to the ground and eating grass, hiding your face in order to stick your finger down your throat and cause yourself to vomit, making yourself belch, even urinating on your attacker. You can act as if you are responding to his demands

(starting to unbutton you blouse) until you can find a point to safely react. Your own ingenuity is your best guide. Crying might be effective in some instances.

- Doing something he doesn't expect may stop or delay him because the rapist wants to be in control and finds it difficult to cope with something he hadn't anticipated. It is doing the unexpected convincingly, so that he doesn't become more antagonistic.

Talking

- The first few minutes you may be too terrified to utter a sound. That's perfectly normal. But if you have thought about the possibility of sexual assault, the shock will not be as great.
- The key to this tactic, which can be successful in aborting an attack, is to speak calmly and sincerely as one human being trying to reach out to another human being. You should not beg, plead, cower or make small talk. Many times this is what your assailant expects to hear and it may antagonize him further. It could range from your pet, a recent movie you've seen, a book you are reading, to a recent death in the family. The range of subject matter is limitless. The important thing in the use of this tactic is to attempt to relate the feeling that you are seeing him as a person.
- Hopefully, convincing him you are seeing him as a person instead of some sort of monster will make him perceive you as an individual offering your concern and not as his enemy.
- You need to make him see that you are not an object on which to vent his anger.
- You should make an effort to reduce his rage by enhancing his ego. Try to gain psychological advantage over him. Don't give him a sermon. He may be trying to rape you because he thinks women are too uppity and it would give him great satisfaction to knock a moralizing female

down. To his way of thinking, if he can pull you down, it raises his self-esteem. That's why it is extremely important to try to reach him in a way that will break his fantasy and allow him to see you as an individual (not an object) with honest feelings and concerns.

- If something you are saying is antagonizing him further, switch to another topic, as quickly and smoothly as you can.

Fighting

- When considering this tactic, you should keep in mind that all rapists have the potential for inflicting serious harm—they are all potentially violent.
- This is probably the last tactic to try if all others have failed. If you start out by fighting you will have little or no opportunity to try any other way because you are already committed to this behavior.
- If using this tactic you must be willing and able to inflict serious injury on your assailant.
- Surprise and speed of reaction should be used to your benefit. If you use a fighting tactic that will not completely incapacitate, you are probably going to be in worse shape.
- If you try to fight him and he has a weapon, always assume that he won't hesitate to use it.
- Your risks of receiving serious injury from your assailant are greatly increased when using such tactics as biting, scratching, pounding his chest with your fists, trying to spray mace or hair spray into his eyes or using any other weapon that will not completely incapacitate him.

Remember...

If you are going to fight your attacker, use surprise and speed to your advantage. For instance, gently put your hands on the assailant's face and get you thumbs near his eyes, then press his eyeballs suddenly with your thumbs as hard as you can. This will put the assailant into shock and could blind him. Or grab his testicles (not his penis, since it will not be effective) squeeze as hard as you can and jerk or pull to inflict immobilizing pain. Both of these tactics can be accomplished in such a way that the assailant is not aware of your plans for a physical attack. If used, they must be sure and quick and you must be willing to follow through to insure the disabling injury of the assailant.

Tactics and precautions are meant to be suggestions and guidelines. The prevention material presented here can reduce your chances of being sexually assaulted and, through awareness and understanding, increase your chances of avoiding or surviving a sexual assault.

There is not a universal prescription for avoiding a sexual assault. You will have to decide which tactic will be most likely to be effective depending on the situation, what type of person you are and who you perceive your assailant to be.

If You Are Sexually Assaulted

Your immediate concern will be in obtaining proper medical and psychological help. This help is readily available. (See Web site reference guide.) Call the police, whether or not you decide to later prosecute. As soon as possible, police will take you to a hospital or rape center.

If you do not want to call the police, at least contact a physician or crisis center. These persons can offer some objective professional advice about the situation to help decide how to proceed.

Police sensitivity to the trauma of the victim and the investigative procedures to enhance the possibility of conviction of the suspect have improved greatly over the last few years.

Even though it may be your initial impulse, *don't douche, shower, change clothes or disturb the crime scene.*

At first, prosecution may be the last thing on your mind but after your initial needs are met you will probably want to assist the police. So be sure you don't destroy any valuable physical evidence.

If you decide to call the police and report the crime, they will ask you some initial questions regarding the identity and location of the suspect, his direction of flight and whether he had a weapon. These questions may be asked en route to the hospital or crisis center.

Procedures differ among hospitals, but basically you will be asked general questions. Name, date of birth, brief medical history and perhaps some other general information. You will first be checked and treated for any visible physical injuries. It should be pointed out any treatment you receive will be strictly at your option. A complete internal examination will be performed, evidence gathered, photographs taken and specimen collected. You will be offered medication to prevent venereal disease or pregnancy. You will not be given any medication to which you object.

Usually, if your physical and mental condition permit, you will be asked to give a formal statement as soon as possible.

Should you decide to prosecute, the state attorney's office will handle the case. They will prosecute if they feel they have enough evidence.

Remember you are not on trial—the defendant is. But under the criminal justice system he is assumed innocent until proven guilty.

In many areas, help is available for victims with questions or doubts about prosecution from: state attorney's office, victim advocate programs, victim witness liaison, rape crisis centers, rape treatment centers and women's groups.

Remember there is no more reason for you to feel guilt, shame or embarrassment than if you had been the victim of any other crime. You were the innocent victim. There are a great many people who are sensitive to your needs and are eager and able to help you.

Appendix II: Resource Guide

Web sites

My Web site
www.UndyingWill.com

www.Soar99.org
Speaking Out About Rape

www.Phoenix-Center.50megs.com
Southwest Florida Rape Trauma
Center, Inc.

www.rainn.org
Rape, Abuse and Incest National
Network

www.saferoom.org
The Saferoom Project

www.fcasv.org
Florida Council Against Sexual
Violence

www.vaw.umn.edu
Violence Against Women office

www.ncvc.org
National Center for Victims
of Crime

www.ywca.org
YWCA

www.stephanieroper.org
The Stephanie Roper Com-
mittee and Foundation, Inc.
for Victims' Rights

www.try-nova.org
National Organization for
Victim Assistance

www.nsvrc.org
National Sexual Violence
Resource Center

www.actabuse.com
Abuse Counseling and
Treatment

Appendix III:
Living With Trauma

ROXANN SANGIACOMO, M.D.

Many of us are fortunate to come into this world in a safe, nurturing environment. We come to expect that the world will stay this way. When humans are exposed to life-threatening trauma, trust and safety are abolished. Confidence in oneself, others and the environment is lost.

Imagine sitting in your living room while it's raining outside only to have your home blow away around you two minutes later. Or driving out for a burger only to spend six months in a hospital and rehab after being broadsided by a drunken driver. Or maybe going to sleep one night thinking about the vacation you'll be starting the next morning and being awakened by a smoke detector, losing your home and a loved one in the fire. Or as in Donna's case, going to work, planning an outing with her mom the next weekend and worrying about making her car payment, only to be fighting for her life a few hours later.

The cluster of symptoms known as post-traumatic stress disorder (PTSD) do not occur simultaneously any more than a baby goes from lying still to running. It is a cascade. As the trauma survivor ventures back out into the old safe environment, he or she gradually develops a keen eye for potentially harmful situations. Calm is lost. Ease is lost. Confidence is gone. Anxiety increases. Sights, smells, sounds each need to be evaluated one at a time. Details must be checked out individually. Viewing the environment as a big picture isn't safe. Something might be missed, and it's that little detail that got missed before that the survivor feels got them into trouble in the first place. "If only I had…. If only I hadn't…then…."

In living through and with a personal trauma, either physical, emotional or both, the strong human instinct of responsibility fosters guilt; and guilt comes in many forms. Guilt at putting one's family and friends through an emotional situation, guilt at being different than one was in the past, guilt at letting oneself down and the guilt of having caused the trauma, as in Donna's assault. She carried the guilt that she caused her attack by going to her attacker's car to help him. Her guilt continued for 15 years until she heard from her attacker's own lips he harmed her because he "had the opportunity" to do so.

Fortunately for her, she was at an emotional place where hearing this made sense, and closure on that aspect of the trauma was achieved.

Unfortunately, for many trauma survivors, that closure never comes. The secondary victims (friends, family, coworkers) of PTSD continue to feed the guilt/shame of the survivor through their words and actions. They fail to understand that the victim didn't want to be a victim. The victim had no choice. But those around them, in a way, do have a choice. By detaching from the victim, downplaying the trauma, urging the victim to "get over it" or "get on with your life," family and friends are insulating themselves, protecting themselves. They don't want to give up their sense of safety, security, trust and confidence that they would have to give up if they acknowledged that this terrible thing happened to someone they know and could happen to them. If they do, they will lose what the victim lost. They don't want to lose their ease, their calm, their confidence, so they push the victim to act "normal," as before. Everyone becomes frustrated, and the victim is again victimized.

Recovery from trauma is a process that may never be complete but one that must have a beginning. The journey begins with acceptance by the survivor of the trauma and by supporters that the trauma was a life-altering event for both. Recovery is like making a gourmet meal; it involves planning, referencing recipes used by others, maybe consulting a well-seasoned chef. There is a lot of hard work and maybe even some regrets about how things should have come out versus how they did.

Recovery is a journey, and it will be trial and error for most. Using what works, discarding what doesn't, changing behaviors, adding supporters and moving away from those who revictimize due to their own ignorance. If what you are doing isn't working, do something else!

Trauma has many causes and PTSD, many faces. All cases come from the loss of sense of safety in our environment and trust in others and ourselves. I don't believe it can ever be restored to a pretrauma level; innocence, once lost, is never regained. But confidence can be rebuilt.

As a board-certified psychiatrist, certainly I recommend therapy, education about trauma, possibly medication and self-help books as part of standard treatment. But I also recommend each person access these tools at his or her own pace, not at the pace that is comfortable for those around them. The process of recovery may take 10, 20 or even 30 years, and it may not be continuous. Look to others like you and "salt to taste."

Give the Gift of
Undying Will
to Your Friends and Colleagues

CHECK YOUR LEADING BOOKSTORE OR ORDER HERE

❑ **YES**, I want _____ copies of *Undying Will* at $13.00 each, plus $4.95 shipping per book (Florida residents please add $.78 sales tax per book). Canadian orders must be accompanied by a postal money order in U.S. funds. Allow 15 days for delivery.

❑ **YES**, I am interested in having Donna J. Ferres speak or give a seminar to my company, association, school, or organization. Please send information.

My check or money order for $_____ is enclosed.

NAME _____

ORGANIZATION _____

ADDRESS _____

CITY/STATE/ZIP _____

PHONE_____ E-MAIL _____

Please make your check payable and return to:
Sago Publishing
12328 Honeysuckle Road
Fort Myers, FL 33912